ASSET STRUCTURE AND SAVING BEHAVIOUR OF CULTIVATORS

Asset Structure and Saving Behaviour of Cultivators
A Study

By

Ram Murti Sharma

ANMOL PUBLICATIONS PVT. LTD.
NEW DELHI - 110 002 (INDIA)

ANMOL PUBLICATIONS PVT. LTD.
4374/4B, Ansari Road, Daryaganj
New Delhi - 110 002

Asset Structure and Saving Behaviour of Cultivators

First Edition, 2000

ISBN 81-261-0663-8

PRINTED IN INDIA

Published by J.L. Kumar for Anmol Publications Pvt. Ltd., New Delhi - 110 002 and Printed at Mehra Offset Press, Delhi.

Contents

Preface

Since agriculture is the pivot of the Haryana economy, it is quite important to analyse how this sector of the economy has been affected by general growth process and, more importantly, how it has in turn affected the overall growth process. Present study focus on the income and asset structure and saving investment behaviour of the cultivator households in Haryana. It would help to evaluate the inner mechanic of the growth process in this sector as also to work out its inter-relation with the rest of the state economy in growth centre context.

The study is substantially based on my research work leading to Ph.D. degree at Kurukshetra University, under the supervision of Dr. C.B. Sharma. I am deeply beholden to him for his inspiration and encouragement. His comments have been of immense value. I also received constant encouragement and suggestions from Prof. S. Kaushil, Professor T.R. Kundu and Dr. Mohinder Paul my sincere thanks to all of them.

In shaping the study into present form, detailed and incisive comments of the Anmol Publications Pvt. Ltd. have been of great value both in analysis and in editing.

Dr. Ram Murti

List of Tables

1

Introduction

Soon after Haryana came into existence as a separate State on November 1, 1966, specific plans and programmes were initiated for the rapid development of this region which had till then been relatively a backward region. As a consequence of these action plans and programmes, the state came to achieve a remarkable pace of growth and climbed rapidly along the growth ladder to reach the second top rung among the states in terms of the per capita product.

The state economy is dominated by the agricultural sector which contributes more than 50 percent to the state domestic product while nearly 80 percent of the total population derives its livelihood from agriculture directly and indirectly. As a result of the technological break through and infrastructure facilities built up by the state government, additional incomes are being generated in this sector of the economy. As a matter of fact, the status of the state in terms of per capita income owes to the relatively rapid increase in the average income of the cultivator households which has shown an average increase of 11.39 percent per annum over the 1966-90 period. Since agriculture is the pivot of the state economy, it is quite important to analyse in some detail how this sector of the economy has been affected by general growth process and, more importantly, how it has in turn affected the overall growth process. In the present study, we shall focus on the income and asset-structure and the saving-investment behaviour of that cultivator households. Such analysis would help us evaluate the inner mechanics of the growth process in this sector as also to work out its inter-relation with the rest of the state economy in a growth-centric context.

Economy is directly related and dependent upon three important factors income, saving and investment which are interlinked. For economic development, investment plays a vital role and is a necessary condition, but there can be no investment without saving. On the otherhand there can be no saving without income. Our past investment becomes the present level of income. To increase the stock of capital goods, we shall have to take stock of saving; as it is the variable with the help of which an economic unit can expect a higher level of growth and consumption.

The total savings (or investment) of a country are generally identified as originating from the following three distinct saver groups: (i) individuals (households), (ii) corporate, and (iii) the government. Admittedly, none of these sectors is a homogeneous whole; each one is a amalgam of rather heterogeneous units. However, as among the three categories, there is ample heterogeneity to make the categorization analytically meaningful. Thus, the household sector includes farm households, unicorporated business enterprises (sole proprietorship or partnership) engaged in manufacturing, trading and other types of business activity and other households engaged in services in the farm and non-farm sectors. The saving propensities of different household sub-groups together with their income shares determine the contribution of the total household sector to total saving/investment. The present study is limited to the cultivator households sub-group of the individual (or households) group.

Concept of Saving

The aggregate volume of savir.gs for individuals during any period is usually defined as the difference between their current income and current expenditures, the latter includes personal tax payments as well as consumption expenditures. This is the income-account approach to saving. Alternatively, one may define saving as the change in earned surplus or earned net worth of an economic unit or individual. In other words, saving is equal to change in assets and liabilities adjusted for capital losses/gains and revaluation of assets and transfers. This is the balance-sheet approach to saving. Thus, for determining savings, one may follow either the income-account approach or balance-sheet approach.

However, the merit of the balance-sheet approach is that it enables us to determine savings of an economic unit directly and more accurately on the basis of the information regarding investment (the 'uses-of-funds' statement) and resource mobilization (the 'source-of-funds' statement). The income-account approach involves obtaining information about saving through income and consumption. The longer the period for which savings are to be estimated, the more difficult it becomes to obtain information regarding consumption expenditures and income, particularly when the economic unit in question is almost illiterate, as is the position in the case of most of the cultivators. Also, the investment behaviour remains divorced from the saving behaviour. The balance-sheet approach, in contrast, presents an integrated view of saving and investment behaviour. The present study, therefore, employs the balance-sheet approach.

Composition of Saving

The difference between current income and expenditure during an accounting year is called saving. It may be in different forms such as increase in cash and securities or reduction in debts, increase in insurance or the investment in long term and short term undertakings or movable goods. Hence, it does not mean that saving always and necessarily increases the liquid assets of an individual or unit as some part of the saving may have been invested into non-liquid assets during an accountable period.

The identification of critical components of financial as well as of physical savings (in the form of assets) is necessary so as to increase and channelize the cultivator house-holds' savings for the overall development of the economy. Savings take different forms, financial and non-financial, and a comprehensive analysis of it is essential to know about their relative magnitudes as well as inter-relationships among them. The components[1] of financial assets usually are:

(i) bank deposits,

(ii) share and securities,

(iii) small saving/postal saving,

(iv) life-insurance premia,

(v) contribution to provident fund, and

(vi) purchase of gold and jewellery.

According to a household survey of income, saving and consumer expenditure carried out by the NCAER[2], contractual savings do not carry much weight in the rural areas, for two reasons : (i) most of the rural income is generated from agricultural activities where contractual savings in the form of life insurance and provident funds have no relevance, and (ii) low income on account of small holdings generally forces them to prefer land improvement, etc., to insurance.

One of the significant components of financial saving in the rural economy is bank deposits[3]. If this component, alongwith small savings, is properly activated, it may play an important role in the mobilisation of resources. Insurance of crops, on the other hand, may also provide incentive for savings in the financial form.

The alternative form of savings, i.e., physical savings, plays an important role in rural sector in enhancing production. The residential property including house-sites, machinery, live-stock, implements, cattle-sheds and other durable have particular importance in increasing agricultural production and thus agricultural income. Let us say the savings in physical assests are more important than the savings in financial assests.

Objectives of the Study

The main purpose of this study is to analyse the data on income, saving and investment of cultivators in Haryana which determine in a major way the nature and intensity of the region's economic performance and problems. It is hoped that this type of study at the micro level would provide some useful guidelines to the practical policy makers.

The main objectives of the present study may briefly be stated as follows:

1. To collect data on asset, income, savings and investment of cultivators (large, medium and small) in Haryana State.

2. To make estimates of aggregate income, assets, savings and investment in the State on the basis of these data.

3. To study in depth the sources and composition of income, savings and investment of cultivators in Haryana.

4. To find out the section of the cultivators which accounts for the maximum savings, the form their savings usually take, and the saving propensities of the different categories of cultivators.

5. To find out and specify the various demographic and socio-economic parametres characterizing the different categories of cultivators and, more importantly, influencing their saving decisions.

In short, the study aims at estimating and analysing the quantum and composition of saving, investment,assets and incomes of the different categories of cultivator households in Haryana during the reference period.

Concepts, Methodology and Sample Design

Important concepts, methodology and sample design used in the study are as follows:

1. Household

Household is the basic unit taken for the purpose of sampling and analysis of the data collected for the study. It is defined as a group of persons related by blood, marriage or adoption, sharing a common kitchen. Accordingly, even a single person may be considered as constituting a household if a kitchen is maintained by him. New-born babies and brides coming into the household are counted as the members of the household irrespective of the duration of their stay with the household as the one responsible for taking major financial decisions has been taken as the head of the household.

2. Reference period

A fixed one year period has been adopted as the reference period for the collection of data relating to household asset structure, saving, income, investment and other related variables. The reference period corresponds to the agricultural year, 1989-90.

3. Earner

An earner is defined as a person who depends for his livelihood on his own employment income, or property income, or a combination of such incomes. Persons receiving pensions or contributions are not considered as earners. Family members actively engaged or helping in the farming business, professions or craft have been considered as earners even if no seperate income is reported by them.

4. Gross Income

Gross income of a household has been defined as a flow of receipts net of expenses incurred in the process of production during the reference period. Gross receipts are so defined as to include all receipts of the household relating to production activity in which its members are engaged. The various sources of income to a cultivator household identified in the survey are as follows:

(a) Income or earnings from farm and non-farm enterprises.

(b) Wages and salaries (if farmer/member is engaged partly in any other work).

(c) Property income (rent, interest and dividends).

(d) Pensions and regular contributions (transfer payment or transfer income).

Gross income includes the rental value of owneroccupied houses. But capital gains and losses and irregular transfer receipts such as gifts, dowries and irregular lump-sum receipts from matured insurance policies, provident fund, chit funds, lottery, prizes, etc., are not included in current income.

Gross income from farm enterprises and allied activities is defined as the value of all farm output less value of current expenses incurred for its production and sale. Farm income includes an adjustment for the imputed value of farm produce retained for household consumption. The value of the output (of crop) is derived as follows: If a farmer has not sold any part of his output, the entire output has been valued at the farm harvest prices. If a farmer has sold a part of his output/produce and retained the other, then actual value of the part sold plus the imputed value of retained output is taken as the total value of his produce and is valued accordingly. In the case of by-products, value as indicated by the farmers has been computed. From the gross produce thus obtained, operating expenses (i.e. cost of seeds, fertilizers, manures, hired labour, irrigation charges, marketing charges, land revenue and the rents paid for leased lands etc.) have been deducted. Repairs and maintenance expenditures form a part of operating expenses because they are needed to maintain capital stock in working condition during the production year. In the case of animal husbandry and other agricultural activities, the gross income has been obtained by deducting the operating expenses from the value of output during the reference period.

If the farmer is working as a labourer during the season/off season, wages earned from agricultural and non-agricultural employment have been included in the gross income. The data on wages includes both the cash receipts as well as the imputed value of payments received in kind (such as meals, tea, biri, etc.). Income from salaries received by the members of the farm household includes the basic pay, allowances, bonus, and other fringe benefits, if any. In some cases, it is rather difficult to draw a distinction between salaried and wage-earning jobs. We have thus taken the income derived from white colour jobs as incomes from salaries.

Gross income earned by members of a farm household who are self-employed in non-farming activities such as business, crafts and professions has been computed by deducting the operating expenses incurred by them. Gross income from self-employment in non-farming includes cash as well as credit sales and receipts in kind, money equivalent of withdrawals for home consumption being duly adjusted for. Receipts in kind are more popular and important in our rural economy because payments by farmers to village artisans like barbers, blacksmiths, etc. are still normally made in kind. Business operating expenses relate to raw material costs, wages and salaries paid, expenses of storage, marketing and transportation, repair, taxes and duties. While determining income, all the details of household earnings and operating expenses have been taken into consideration.

Rental income from tenants, interest and dividends, and gross receipts from property are also the source of income of a cultivator household. Gross income from property is derived by deducting the current expenses incurred for maintenance of the residential buildings including house tax, if any, paid from the income which includes actual rent received by the household and imputed value of the rental income of the house owned and occupied by the household. Income received by the members of the household from other sources such as interest, dividends, pensions and regular contributions are obtained directly through appropriate questions included in the schedule canvassed during the survey. Irregular remittances and windfall receipts from lotteries, etc., if any are treated as capital transfers received by the household and not as a part of current income. In this study, income from rental value of own residential buildings is taken as 6 per cent of its value.

5. *Net-Income*

Net income is defined as gross income minus depreciation.

6. *Depreciation*

Depreciation, representing used up value of the income yielding physical assets during the reference period, is estimated for building, property, business and farm assets. There are several problems involved in the methods of estimation of depreciation but all are essentially based on value and life of an asset. Depreciation is estimated on the basis of replacement value of physical assets and their expected life span. The rates of depreciation vary from asset to asset depending on the nature and age of assets. The following rates of depreciation have been applied while calculating the depreciation in the case of different assets.

Sr.No.	Items/Assets	Rate of Depreciation (per cent per annum)
1.	Bullocks	12
2.	Wells	3
3.	Building (a) Pucca	2.5
	(b) Kacha	5
4.	Iron persian wheel and chains	25
5.	Other parts	10
6.	Oil engine	15
7.	Electric Motor	10
8.	Boring	10
9.	Cart	10
10.	Fodder Cutter	20
11.	Gur Boiling Pan	10
12.	Improved Ploughs	10
13.	Cane crasher	10
14.	Thrasher	7
15.	Karaha/Sohaga	25
16.	Cultivator/Tiller/Plough	10
10.	Seed Drill	7
18.	Harrow	10
19.	Offset Desi Plough	10
20.	Trolly/Trailor	10
21.	Leveller/Karaha	25
22.	Seed-drills	7

Source: *Farm Accounts in Punjab 1987-88*, Publication No. 592, Economic and Statistical Organisation, Punjab, Chandigarh.

7. *Investment*

In this study, investment by a household has been broadly classified into two categories:

(a) Investment in physical assets, and

(b) Investment in financial assets.

Investment in consumer durables has also been included in the investment in physical assets. Investment in physical assets comprises investment expenditure on land (including land improvements and purchase of land), agricultural implements and machinery (including purchase or construction of means of irrigation and purchase of other types of farm machinery), cattle sheds, live-stocks, etc. Investment in business assets include additions made to existing business and other improvements made in the business premises, etc. Investment made by a household during the period under study is measured as net value of assets (new assets purchased minus old assets sold). No account has been taken of either the capital gains or losses on the assets possessed by a household due to an increase or decrease in their prices. Gross investment in physical assets has, therefore, been measured as the change in these assets due to additions and improvements made to the existing stock. Investment in live-stock is arrived at by net purchase of live-stock (i.e., purchase minus sale) during the period under study.

The imputed value of family labour employed in investment for permanent land improvements has also been included by adopting the method used by the NCAER[4]. Investment in consumer durables includes bicycles, motor-cycles/scooters, radios, television sets, sewing machines, domestic appliances and household furniture, etc.

Investment in financial assets consists of net purchase of shares and securities, increase in bank deposits, small savings (postal savings), premium paid for life insurance and provident fund contributions. It also includes purchase of gold and silver.

8. Saving

The term saving denotes the residual of current income after appropriation for current consumption expenditure irrespective of whether this residual is in the form of cash or kind, in physical or financial assets. Savings may take a variety of forms, including the increase in cash and securities and net addition to durable assets and inventories. However, the income-accounting approach, which estimates savings by deducting consumption from income, has certain limitations. In a family budget inquiry, the emphasis primarily is on consumption expenditure while the income side is rather neglected, so that there is a general tendency for consumption expenditures to be over estimated and income to be under estimated. Further, it does not highlight the various forms of investment in which savings are embodied. Recourse has, therefore, taken to the balance sheet method, which has two main reasons for being preferred in this respect: In the first place, the margin of error inherent in the balance-sheet method is less than that in the income-account method. Secondly, the estimated of saving derived by this method are more informative as they also reflect the manner in which it is utilised by the households. In India, both the National Council of Applied Economic Research (NCAER) and the Reserve Bank of India make use of the balance-sheet method for estimating household saving. For the purpose of present study, while the balance-sheet approach has been adopted, especially for estimating saving, some useful information on items of consumption during the reference period has also been convassed through the schedule.

Thus, the saving is taken as a change in the earned net worth and has been computed as the difference between the change in the value of assets and change in the value of liabilities adjusted for net capital transfers. The saving of a household during the accounting period may be expressed as:

$$S = (\Delta A_p + \Delta A_f) - (\Delta L + T)$$

where S = Cultivator household saving,

ΔA_p = Change in physical assets (acquisitions minus liquidations),

ΔA_f = Change in financial assets (increase minus decreases),

ΔL = Change in liabilities (increase in borrowings minus increase in lending), and

T = Net inflow of capital transfers (inflow minus outflow)

Net capital gains or losses due to appreciation or depreciation in the value of assets have been ignored.

9. Net Saving

Net saving has been taken as gross saving less allowances for depreciation. Correspondingly, we define net investment as gross investment minus depreciation. Depreciation represents used up value of income-yielding physical assets during the reference period. It has been estimated for buildings, business and farm assets excluding land used for live-stock.

10. Liabilities

Liabilities of a household include all claims against the household such as amount of loan, mortgage on house/property and overdrafts from banks.

11. Assets

Assets have been taken to signify the total wealth (worth) of a household. Assets have been divided into two parts: (a) Physical and (b) Financial. Physical assets refer to and include the stock of buildings (residential and other property), land including vacant house sites, live-stock, implements and machinery and consumer durables. The choice of items to be included as assets is based on the durability and purpose of assets. The shorter the time period intended for study, the shorter the life of assets that need to be included in saving. As the present study is confined to a period of one year, it has been decided to include all physical assets which last more than a year. The financial assets include shares, deposits, gold and silver and dues receivable in cash and kind owned by a household.

Methodology and Sample Design

The present study is related to the cultivator households in the State of Haryana. The area defined for the purpose of the survey comprises all the inhabited villages covered under the 1981 census. The study is based on the cross-section data which was specifically collected for the purpose through the cluster survey method with the help of a pre-tested schedule specially designed for collecting comprehensive information. A three-stage stratified proportionate random sampling technique was adopted for the selection of districts, villages and the ultimate sample cultivator households.

At the first stage, four districts were selected, one each from the four agro-climatic zones into which the various districts were grouped according to their respective agro-climatic conditions. The first zone consists of Ambala, Karnal and Kurukshetra districts, while the second includes the districts of Sonepat,Jind and Rohtak. The third zone comprises the Hissar, Sirsa and Bhiwani districts, and the fourth comprises the districts of Faridabad, Gurgaon and Mehandergarh. From each zone, one district was selected, i.e. district Ambala from zone One, Jind from zone Two, Hissar from zone Three and Faridabad from zone Four. The sample has thus been fairly representative of the different sub-regions of the state.

At the second stage, out of the four selected districts, two villages were selected from each. Out of these two villages one was selected within a radius of 10 Km. from the district Headquarter. It was well equipped with the facilities such as High School, Bank, Post-Office,

Co-operative Society, etc. The second village was within a radius of 30 to 40 Kms. from the district Headquarter and deprived of the infrastructure facilities as mentioned earlier. In this way these eight villages were selected to represent inter district variations. In this study-context, all the sixteen districts should have been given representation to make it an ideal situation, but shortage of time, paucity of funds and other technical and practical considerations stood in the way.

At the third stage, all the sample cultivator households in the selected villages were listed and classified into three categories of large farmers, medium farmers and small farmers depending upon the operational area of their holdings. Farmers operating upto 5 acres of land were classified as small, while those operating between 5 and 10 acres were classified as medium. Those with operational holdings of above 10 acres were classified as large farmers. In the context of the study of the eight selected villages, the household population was taken in such a way as to make a total of 1600 households. It was at random sample of households (45 households from each village) and each village was given equal representation in the already explained three categories of cultivator households.

In the present study, every effort has been made to avoid as far as possible, the non-sampling errors. The purpose and the need of the study were explained to the respondents and enough confidence was generated among them so as to make them willing truthfully to reveal their financial position. Whenever a household was found to be non-cooperative or its responses not credible it was dropped from the sample. In all, forty households and thus to be dropped from the sample. The reasons for non-response were mainly non-availability of the respondents at home, non-cooperation and complete refusal.

The category-wise distribution of the cultivators in

the four selected districts of Haryana State as in 1988-89 has been shown in Table 1.1.

Table 1.1
Category-wise Percentage Distribution of the Cultivators in Selected Districts

Type of Cultivators	District's Percentage			
	Hissar	Faridabad	Jind	Ambala
(a) Small Farmers	46.6	71.4	47.7	63.3
(b) Medium Farmers	23.3	16.6	26.6	19.8
(c) Large Farmers	30.1	12.0	27.7	16.9
Total	100	100	100	100

Source: Statistical Abstract of Haryana, 1988-89, Economic and Statistical Organisation, Chandigarh, 1989.

On the basis of above percentage of cultivators in the different districts, the sample of 320 (80 from each district) households were selected. Out of 320 sample households, 183 were small farmers, 66 medium farmers and 71 large farmers. The percentage of non-respondent cultivators among the different categories has been shown in Table 1.2. The number of non-respondents was the highest in the case of medium farmers (13.15). It was 11.16 for small farmers and 8.97 per cent for large farmers.

Table 1.2
Non-Respondents classified by type of Households

Type of Cultivator Households	Number of Household Selected	Number of Non-respondents	Percentage of Non-respondents
1	2	3	4
(a) Large Farmers	78	7	8.97
(b) Medium Farmers	76	10	13.15
(c) Small Farmers	206	23	11.16
Total	360	40	11.11

Table 1.3
Distribution of the Selected Households District-wise and Category-wise

Districts	Small Farmers	Medium Farmers	Large Farmers	Total
1	2	3	4	5
Hisar	38	18	24	80
Faridabad	57	13	10	80
Jind	38	19	23	80
Ambala	50	16	14	80
Total	183	66	71	320

The size-wise composition of the sample households in the State is similar to that making our sample a representation sample.

Limitations of the Study

Special care has been taken to minimise the possible errors. About three months were devoted to the collection of the necessary information from the 320 households. Reliability of data depends, among other things, on the skill, efficiency and preservance of the interviewer and the appropriateness of the form and contents of the questionnaire from the point of view of relevance, manageability and feasibility. With a view to acquiring the necessary skill and judging the manageability and feasibility of the questionnaire, a tentative schedule of questions was framed and administered as a trial to 6 households, 2 households being taken from each category. The questionnaire was suitably modified in the light of the experience gained from these trial cases.

Studies based on the primary survey method have their own problems and limitations. The present study is no exception in this regard, one major limitation of the study has been that data on the various items of financial savings such as cash in hand, purchase of gold and jewellery and amount deposited with bank, etc., are not the true reflection of the situation. The respondents in many cases have been found to have had a feeling of fear or suspicion or indifference while giving necessary information on these. This is generally true of people any where in India; but it is more so of people in rural parts who are mostly illiterate and not used to such verbal encounters. Inspite of having made our best efforts and having taken all feasible precaution, we can only claim to have lessened the extent of this limitation; we cannot claim to have eliminated it altogether. By explaining to such unwieldy respondents the nature and purpose of the survey time and again and by seeking the intervention of their relatively more enlightened fellow respondents, necessary information could be elicited from them.

Secondly, some degree of arbitrariness cannot be avoided while deciding about the questions of the longevity of the assets, the rate of depreciation and the current valuation of assets. Apart from these difficulties, the partially monetised business of the rural households posed an additional problem of imputed values which are subjective. In order to tackle this problem, cross questions were put to the respondents to check the reliability of the values of the non-marketed produce imputed by them.

The asset accumulation behaviour was thus assessed but it still lacked dynamic content. The probable questions which might arise are:

Study of the behaviour of the cultivators is incomes, expenditures and savings; the effects of Govt. rural development programmes on the economic conditions of the farmers; and other related questions. An adequate analysis cannot be completed (composed) for want of a dynamic setting. In the present study cross-section analysis was emphasized but it could not bring conformatory results owing to certain constraints in collecting time series data and other resources limitations.

The use of some of the quantitative techniques has been made. The quantitative techniques used are: concentration ratio, coefficient of variation, standard deviation of logarithms and Theil index. The utility and limitations of these techniques are discussed in Chapter Two.

Chapterization

The study has been divided into four chapters. Chapter One assumes the introduction and accordingly spells out the concepts, methodology and sample design, and important objective of the study. Income and asset structure of the various categories of cultivator households has been examined in Chapter Two. Chapter three deals with the saving and investment behaviour of the cultivator households and examines the volume, pattern and determinants of saving and investment. The major findings flowing from the study alongwith some important suggestions for policy implications have been presented in Chapter Four.

References

1. National Council of Applied Economic Research (NCAER), Report 1972, p. 75.
2. *Ibid.*, p. 33.
3. *Ibid.*, p. 75.
4. National Council of Applied Economic Research (NCAER), Report 1975, pp. 21-22.

2

Income and Asset Structure

The present chapter deals with the income and asset structure of cultivator households in Haryana. For the purpose of our analysis, this chapter has been divided into two sections. Section one examines the composition and distribution of income, while the asset - structure, its composition and distribution have been discussed in section two.

Section I

One of the important aims of this study is to estimate household income, its composition and distribution in one segment of the cultivator household sector. The income of this sector can be briefly defined as the aggregate net value of the goods and services produced by its constituents during the year. The attempt to collect data on income is thus an attempt to embrace, within a single measurable concept, the whole gamut of the household sector's productive activities. By doing so, it is possible to obtain (a) an index of the value of total economic activity, (b) an idea of the variations in such economic activity, and (c) an indication of the relative importance of the different kinds of economic activities. This section is devoted to the presentation of the findings of our study as to the composition of income, distribution of income, the determinants of income and the degree of concentration of income.

For the purpose of present study the sources of

household income have been classified under the following main heads:

(a) agriculture,

(b) live-stock

(c) agricultural and non-agricultural wages,

(d) business crafts and professions,

(e) salaries,

(f) rental income from housing,

(g) interest and dividends and pensions,

(h) current transfers, and

(i) any others.

The concept of gross income from agriculture has been defined as a flow of receipts net of expenses incurred in the process of production. The estimated depreciation attributable to farm assets owned by the cultivators was deducted from gross income to arrive at the net income from agriculture. Wages comprise the earning of persons engaged in agricultural and non-agricultural activities. Income from business, crafts and professions is arrived at by deducting the operating expenses from the gross receipts. The amount of depreciation attributable to business undertaken by the cultivator households in the process of trading, manufacturing, transportation or such other activity was deducted from the gross income to arrive at the net income. In computing the income from household property, both the rental income derived from rented out houses and the imputed rental value of the owner-occupied houses were taken into account. The other items of income include interest and dividends and current transfers. Current transfers are arrived at by deducting the inflows from outflows.

As Goldsmith says, "In any economic calculation, account must be taken not only of the current input of labour and materials but also of the contribution made by durable goods in the form of their gradual physical as well as economic consumption in the process of production. Depreciation allowances are a necessary part of cost. Hence, net income as well as retained income, i.e. saving, must be net of depreciation allowances"[1].

The data on components of income in respect of the different categories of cultivator households are presented in Table 2.1. The table indicates that in the case of large farmers, agriculture constitutes the single most important component of household income, accounting for 64.13 per cent of the total household income of this category followed by 'live-stock' and 'pensions, dividends, interest and others' with 24.01 per cent and 4.00 per cent shares, respectively. All the other components are of a relatively lesser significance. In the case of medium farmers, agriculture constitutes 43.74 percent of the total household income of this category, followed again by 'livestock' and 'salaries' with 32.78 per cent and 8.82 per cent shares, respectively. 'Interest, dividends, pensions, and others' constitute 5.93 per cent share followed by 'business, crafts and professions' constituting 4.84 per cent share in the total income relating to this category. The other two components are of relatively lesser significance.

In the case of small farmers, agriculture and livestock are the two important components both having almost equal importance and constitute 35.51 and 33.62 per cent shares, respectively, in this category. 'Salaries' and 'business/crafts/ professions' account for 12.60 per cent and 8.74 per cent, respectively. The contribution of the remaining sources of income in this category is relatively insignificant. Thus, in all the categories of households i.e. large, medium and small farmers, similar pattern is found in the sense that more than 69 percent

Table 2.1
Composition of Cultivator Household Income in Haryana

Source	Large Farmers Amount (in Rs.)	Percentage	Medium Farmers Amount (in Rs.)	Percentage	Small Farmers Amount (in Rs.)	Percentage	All Farmers Amount (in Rs.)	Percentage
1. Agriculture (Farming)	3896793	64.13	1338891	43.74	1873671	35.51	7109355	49.32
2. Live Stock	1458446	24.01	1003495	32.78	1773680	33.62	4235621	29.39
3. Business/Crafts/Professions	124600	2.05	148200	4.84	461200	8.74	734000	5.09
4. Salaries	152400	2.51	270000	8.82	664840	12.60	1087240	7.54
5. Wages	4800	0.08	6600	0.22	140900	2.67	152300	1.06
6. House property	195850	3.22	112280	3.67	215268	4.08	523298	3.63
7. Pension, dividends, interest, current transfers and others	243200	4.00	181500	5.93	146886	2.78	571586	3.97
All sources	6076089	100.00	3060966	100.00	5276445	100.00	14413500	100.00
	(42.15)		(21.24)		(36.61)		(100.00)	

of income is generated from agriculture and livestock. It is, however, interesting to note that while the percentage share of income from agriculture declines when we move from large farmers to medium and small farmers categories, the behaviour of income from live stock shows just the reverse picture, i.e. its share increases when we move from large farmers category of households to medium and to the small farmers category.

So far as the cultivator households as a whole are concerned, nearly 49 per cent of the income is generated from agriculture followed by 29.39 percent from livestock, 7.54 per cent from salaries and 5.09 per cent from business/crafts profession. Contribution made by wages is just 1.06 per cent. If we look at the category-wise break up of the total income of the households, we find that large farmers occupy a predominent place with a 42.15 per cent share in the total income, followed by small farmers (36.61 per cent) and medium farmers (21.24 per cent).

Measurement of Income Inequalities

Now we turn to the next important question : what is the extent of economic concentration in rural Haryana? Though from the foregoing we have already had some idea about the prevailing conditions of income-inequality, a more useful and precise form can be given to this idea if we translate it in terms of the various indicators of economic concentration. It is widely believed that an inverted U-type relationship exists between economic growth and income inequalities, that is, income inequalities tend to increase in the early stages of economic growth, stabilise thereafter for some time and finally decrease. (Kuznets : 1955). It is also believed that income distribution is found to be more unequal in a developed economy.

Admittedly, micro level cross section study cannot be adequate for an indepth analysis on this point a macro level and dynamic study is needed. However, as a second-best alternative, a knowledge of the magnitude of income-inequalities in terms of a series of cross-section studies at various points of time can be of much use for an analysis of this aspect and as a basis for further research and policy making.

Alternative techniques are available for measuring inequality in the distribution of income. Although theoretical studies of income distribution were originally initiated by Pareto, the contribution of Gini (1921) and Lorenz (1905) is of great significance. The works of Gilbert (1942) and Atkinson (1970) are also important in this context. There are also some techniques/measures borrowed from the information theory such as the index developed by Theil (1967). However, it would not be out of place to mention here that no single measure can summarise all the factors in a given distribution of income, as the distribution of income itself depends upon the definition of income, techniques used for obtaining data, type of households covered, definition of the household, etc.

In order to measure inequalities in the distribution of income, five measures/indicators of inequality have been used in this study, namely,

(1) Concentration ratio,

(2) Standard deviation of logarithms of income,

(3) Co-efficient of variation,

(4) Share of bottom and top quintiles,

(5) Theil Index.

Attempts have also been made to highlight their merits and limitations as measures of inequality.

Concentration Ratio

The most widely used measure of inequality of

income and asset distribution is the concentration ratio developed by Gini. It is the ratio of area between the Lorenz curve and the egalitarian line to the area of the triangle below the egalitarian line. The Lorenz curve relates to the cumulative proportion of the income received, assuming that the families are arranged in an ascending order of income. The 'egalitarian line' shows the situation where each family receives the same income. Obviously, the concentration ratio as a measure of inequality has its upper limit as unity and lower limit as zero. If each family receives the same income, the Lorenz curve coincides with the 'egalitarian line' and the concentration ratio assumes zero value. On the other hand, if a single family receives all the incomes, the concentration ratio becomes unity.

The concentration ratio has been computed from the grouped data, using the following formula[2]:

$$CR = 1 - \sum_{i=1}^{n} P_1 (z_i + z_{i-1}),\ z_0 = 0$$

where CR = concentration ratio.

P_i = percentage of households receiving income within or below the ith range.

Z_i = cumulative percentage of income received by these families.

The concentration ratio method is characterized by some major problems and lacunae. Firstly, it is possible for different Lorenz curves to intersect. This implies that significantly different distributions may yield identical ratios. In addition, the concentration ratio insensitive to small percentage changes which may represent large shifts to the lower income classes (Goldsmith, 1959, p. 229, Weiskath, 1920, pp. 303-332; and Sen, 1973, pp. 33-34). Thirdly, the boundaries of perfect equality and inequality are so extreme that changes in the concentration ratio index over time tend to understate any actual gains towards equality (Pechman, 1951, p. 217). The sensitivity of the concentration ratio depends not on the size of income level but on the distribution of population over the income sizes (Sen, 1973, pp. 31-34).

Standard Deviation

The standard deviation of logarithms of income is sensitive to income transferred among the lower categories. It is relatively insensitive to income transferred among the high income-earners (Sen, 1973, pp. 29-34). The standard deviation of logarithms has been computed from the following formula[3]:

$$\sigma = \sqrt{\frac{1}{N}\sum_{i=1}^{N}(\log y_i - \overline{\log y})^2}$$

$$\overline{\log y} = \frac{1}{N}\sum_{i=1}^{N}\log y_i$$

N = total number of individual,

y_i = income of the ith class,

$\overline{\log y}$ = population mean.

The percentage of income received by quintiles of families are computed by arranging the income in an ascending order. The coefficient of variation and the standard deviation of log of income are computed from the ungrouped data rather than from the grouped data which is the usual practice.

Coefficient of Variation

The coefficient of variation is an appropriate measure if one is interested in the absolute differences of incomes and assets. But it is very sensitive to changes in the shape of the frequency distribution of income. Moreover, for the purpose of inequality comparisons, it is of doubious value, depending, as it does, on means. Two distributions with the same standard deviation will yield different co-efficients of variation due to differences in means.

Shares of Quintiles

The shares of the quintiles of families in the total income do not yield a single overall measure. If the shares of the lowest (bottom) and the highest (top) families are considered, the omissions of the influences of items that fall outside the selected ranges is a serious disadvantages of the study of income inequality.

Theil Index

Theil Index is used to measure the inter-sector and intra-sector inequality. For the purposes of decomposition, we also use a measure of inequality that is directly decomposable additively within a group component as also between a group component. Either of Theil's (1967) two measures of inequality would have sufficed, but we have chosen the second measure simply because it makes the compuational burden involved more tractable. The Theil Index has been computed from the following formula[4]:

$$T = \Sigma(1/n)\log(m/y_i)$$

where T = denotes Theil Index,

n = total number of individuals in different classes/groups,

m = mean income for all households, and

y_i = mean income accruing to the ith individual/class.

Theil's (1967) index of inequality is particularly useful for handling grouped as well as raw data for providing explanation for the degree of income/asset inequality. When per capita income in all classes is the same, m/y_i is unity for each group. Thus log m/y_i would be zero, giving the index a value of zero. When all income is attained by one individual or group, index assumes a value of log N, where N is the number of individuals/groups. Because of its aggregate proportion, this measure is particularly useful in that it permits decomposition of the total income inequality into its components.

It is but natural that when the families are divided into a number of sub-groups on the basis of a given characteristics, the average inequality for a particular sub-group is important. Because this would enable one to compare one sub-group with another.

Whereas the Lorenz preference provides only a partial ordering of distributions, measures of income inequality have been devised to provide complete orderings; all of these meaasures, the Gini Index is more widely used. As is now widely recognised that alternative inequality measures do not provide the same ranking of distributions. Yntema (1933) was the first to demonstrate such conflicts in ranking. Conducting an empirical study by means of ten wealth and seven income distributions, he arrived at the conclusion that, although some consistency may be found in the ranking of distributions by certain sub-groups of measures, there is little overall uniformity in the ranking of these distributions. In his study of Puerto Rico, Argentina, and Mexico, Weisskoff (1970) observed that, on the basis of the Gini Index and the standard deviation of logarithms of income, Puerto Rico displayed a more equal distribution of income than did Mexico. When the coefficient of variation was used as a measure of inequality, however, Mexico's income distribution appeared more equal. Atkinson (1970), in summarizing Ranadive's conclusions (1965) argued that the differences in ranking are to contradictory that no clear picture emerges of the relative degree of inequality in advanced and developing countries[5]. Champernowne (1974) conducted a detailed simulation study to judge the relative merits of various inequality measures and concluded that there can be no single 'best' measure.

The various measures used in this study to compute the level of inequality in the distribution of income and assets also do not provide the same ranking and hence we have depended mostly on the concentration ratio. However, the results obtained from the remaining four measures are also given in the relevant Tables and discussed in the text wherever desired necessary.

Income Distribution

Table 2.2 shows the distribution of cultivator households by level of income for each category as well as for all cultivator households taken together. The households falling in the lower income group (i.e., with an annual income upto Rs.30,000) constitute about 62.84 per cent of the total households in the case of small farmers, 15.15 per cent in the case of medium farmers, 1.41 per cent in the case of large farmers, and 39.37 per cent in the case of all cultivator households taken together. Likewise, the medium income group households (with an annual income between Rs. 30001-70000) account for 36.07 per cent in the case of small farmers, 74.24 per cent in the case of medium farmers, 39.44 per cent in the case of large farmers, and 44.69 per cent in the case of total cultivator households. And the households falling in the upper income groups (i.e., with an annual income of above Rs. 70,000) account for 1.09 per cent in the case of small farmers, 10.61 per cent in the case of medium farmers, 59.15 per cent in the case of large farmers, and taken together, the percentage of cultivator households falling in this income group comes to 15.94.

A more comprehensive view of the state of economic disparity can be had by comparing the income shares and the population shares of different groups of households. An inspection of Table 2.2 reveals that :

Table 2.2
Distribution of Cultivator Households by Income Level

Income Level (In Rs.)	Small Farmer	Income	Medium Farmer	Income	Large Farmer	Income	All Farmers	Income
Upto 10000	5 (2.73)	36841 (0.70)	-	-	-	-	5 (1.56)	36841 (0.25)
10001-20000	49 (26.78)	794037 (15.05)	-	-	-	-	49 (15.31)	794037 (5.51)
20001-30000	61 (33.33)	1508321 (28.59)	10 (15.15)	245998 (8.04)	1 (1.41)	28160 (.45)	72 (22.50)	1782479 (12.37)
Sub-total	115 (62.84)	2339199 (44.34)	10 (15.15)	245998 (8.04)	1 (1.41)	28160 (0.46)	126 (39.37)	2613357 (18.13)
30001-40000	34 (18.58)	1165317 (22.08)	19 (28.79)	662342 (21.64)	8 (11.27)	274978 (4.53)	61 (19.06)	2102637 (14.59)
40001-50000	17 (9.29)	761733 (14.44)	18 (27.27)	813819 (26.59)	4 (5.63)	172919 (2.85)	39 (12.19)	1748471 (12.13)
50001-60000	12 (6.56)	649662 (12.31)	7 (10.60)	385711 (12.60)	9 (12.68)	489891 (8.06)	28 (8.75)	1525264 (10.58)
60001-70000	3 (1.64)	197860 (3.75)	5 (7.58)	318231 (10.40)	7 (9.86)	449300 (7.39)	15 (4.69)	965391 (6.70)
Sub-total	66 (36.07)	2774572 (52.58)	49 (74.24)	2180103 (71.23)	28 (39.44)	1387088 (22.83)	143 (44.69)	6341763 (44.00)
70001-80000	1 (0.55)	78368 (1.48)	1 (1.52)	74903 (2.44)	10 (14.08)	753082 (12.39)	12 (3.75)	906353 (6.29)
80001-90000	1 (0.54)	84306 (1.60)	2 (3.03)	172030 (5.62)	12 (16.90)	1013292 (16.68)	15 (4.69)	1269628 (8.81)
90001-Above	-	-	4 (6.06)	387932 (12.67)	20 (28.17)	2894467 (47.64)	24 (7.50)	3282399 (22.77)
Sub-total	2 (1.09)	162674 (3.08)	7 (10.61)	634865 (20.73)	42 (59.15)	4660841 (76.71)	51 (15.94)	5458380 (37.87)
All Income Level	183 (100.00)	5276445 (100.00)	66 (100.00)	3060966 (100.00)	71 (100.00)	6076089 (100.00)	320 (100.00)	14413500 (100.00)

Note: Figures in parantheses indicate percentages.

(i) Among the total cultivator households in Haryana, 39.27 per cent fall in the lower income group and their share in the total cultivator households income is only 18.13 per cent.

(ii) 44.69 per cent of the households figure in the medium income group and they amass as much as 44 per cent of the total cultivator households income.

(iii) 15.94 per cent of the households fall in the upper income group and their share in the total cultivator households income is 37.87 per cent.

(iv) Income disparity is found among all categories of cultivator households. In the case of both the small farmers and the medium farmers, percentage share of income increases as we move from lower income group to middle income group and decreases as we move to higher income group of cultivator households, i.e. 44.34 per cent to 52.58 per cent and 8.04 per cent to 71.23 per cent and decreases to 3.08 per cent and 20.73 per cent in the case of small and medium farmers, respectively. But in the case of large farmers, the percentage share of income has been found to be increasing as we move from lower group to middle and further to higher income group, i.e., from 0.46 per cent to 22.83 per cent and further to 76.71 per cent. In aggregate terms, the percentage share of income increases as we move from lower income group to middle income group and decreases as we move from the middle to the higher income group, i.e., 18.13 per cent to 44 per cent and to 37.87 per cent, respectively.

The distribution of income by deciles among the different categories of cultivator households in the state has been shown in Table 2.3, which indicates that there is considerable inequality in the distribution of income

Table 2.3
Income Distribution of Cultivator Households by Deciles

Decile Group	Large Farmers		Medium Farmers		Small Farmers		All Farmers	
	Percentage share in total income	Cumulative percentage	Percentage share in total income	Cumulative percentage	Percentage share in total income	Cumulative percentage	Percentage share in total income	Cumulative percentage
1st Decile	4.34	4.34	6.34	6.34	4.37	4.37	2.99	2.99
2nd Decile	5.45	9.79	7.34	13.68	5.96	10.33	4.23	7.22
3rd Decile	6.81	16.60	8.29	21.97	6.71	17.04	5.18	12.40
4th Decile	7.83	24.43	8.76	30.73	7.86	24.90	6.16	18.56
5th Decile	8.96	33.39	9.43	40.16	8.52	33.42	7.21	25.77
6th Decile	9.69	43.08	10.20	50.36	9.62	43.04	8.37	34.14
7th Decile	10.27	53.35	10.85	61.21	10.84	53.88	10.03	44.17
8th Decile	11.45	64.80	11.34	72.55	12.31	66.19	12.11	56.28
9th Decile	14.44	79.24	12.78	85.33	14.88	81.07	16.13	72.41
10th Decile	20.76	100.00	14.67	100.00	18.93	100.00	27.59	100.00

both when the cultivator households are taken categorywise and when these are taken together. The bottom qunitile of the cultivator households as a whole get a mere 7.22 per cent of the aggregate income. On the other hand, the top quintile take as much as 43.72 per cent. Among the large farmers, the bottom quintile of the households get only 9.79 per cent of the total income of this group whereas the share of the top quintile is 35.20 per cent. And in the case of the medium farmers, the share of the bottom quintile is 13.68 per cent while that of the top quintile is 27.45 per cent. When we shift our attention to the small farmers, we find that the share of bottom quintile is 10.33 per cent and that of top quintile is 33.81 per cent. These results clearly indicate that income is more evenly distributed among the medium and small farmers as compared to large farmers and the cultivator households taken together. More interestingly, the inequality is greater when all cultivator households are taken together than in each of the three size categories taken separately.

To depict the concentration of income distribution more precisely, four Lorenz curves have been drawn one for each category of the cultivator households and one for all households taken together, and presented in Figures 2.1 to 2.4. The different measures of income inequality are given in Table 2.4. It is evident from the Table that the value of concentration ratio is the highest in the case of all households taken together, being 0.352. Category-wise the values of the concentration ratio are 0.242, 0.135 and 0.232 for the large, medium and small farmers respectively. The values of the concentration ratio shows that there is no consistent relation between the size of the holdings and the degree of intra-size equality of income distribution. Thus, the income is almost equally evenly distributed in the case of the small and the large farmers, whereas it is relatively more evenly distributed in the case of medium farmers as compared to large and small farmers.

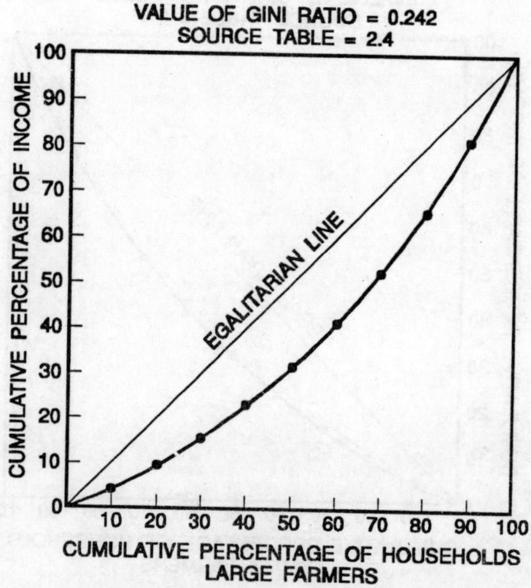

Fig. 2.1. Lorenz Curve Showing Income Inequality

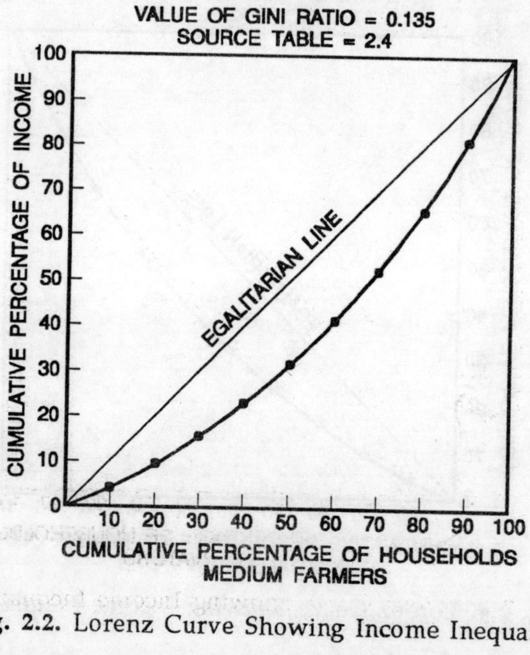

Fig. 2.2. Lorenz Curve Showing Income Inequality

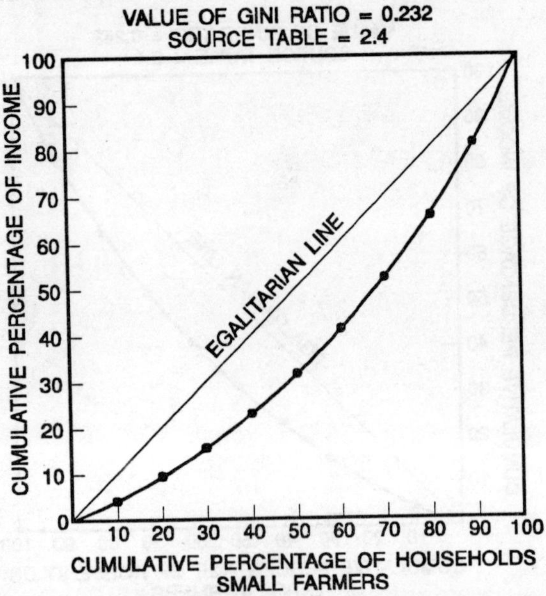

Fig. 2.3. Lorenz Curve Showing Income Inequality

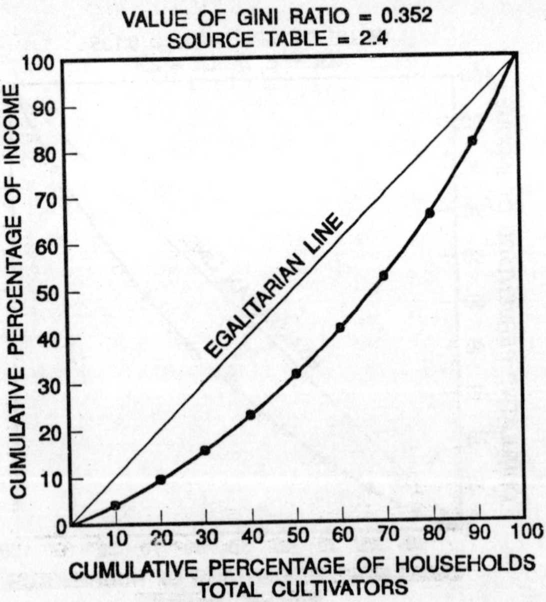

Fig. 2.4. Lorenz Curve Showing Income Inequality

The other measures of inequality such as the coefficient of variation of income, the standard deviation of logarithms of income and the Theil Index of income, more or less, seem to confirm these results.

Table 2.4
Indicators of Income Inequality by Category of Cultivator Households

Inequality Indicators	Large Farmers	Medium Farmers	Small Farmers	Total Farmers
1. Concentration Ratio	0.242	0.135	0.232	0.35
2. Share of botton Quintile (%)	9.79	13.68	10.33	7.22
Share of Top Quintile (%)	35.20	27.45	33.81	43.72
3. Coefficient of Variation of Income (%)	17.50	13.21	17.42	20.73
4. Standard Devition of Logarithms of Income	.330	.192	.214	.356
5. Theil Index	.015	.109	.111	.120

According to an estimate by the NCAER (1980) the Lorenz ratio for the all-India rural households (category) was found to be 0.388, which is higher than the ratio found by our study (i.e. 0.352) for cultivator households in Haryana. This could partly be due to the specific characteristics of the state/region and partly by the difference in sample covered by the two studies.

We shall now analyse the contribution/impact of various factors, such as age and educational level of chief earner, size of the cultivator household, number of earners, etc., on the income of cultivator households.

Age of Chief-Earner

Age of an individual does normally bear significantly upon the earning profiles of individuals. For households comprising many individuals, therefore the average age or the age composition of the household would influence the household's income profile. How-

Table 2.5 (i)

Distribution of Cultivator Households by income level and age of the Chief Earner

Income Level (In Rs.)	Age upto 25 years		Age between 26-30 years		Age between 31-35 years		Age between 36-40 years		Age between 41-45 years	
	Number	Amount	Number	Amount	Number	Amount	Number	Amount	Number	Amount
Upto-10000	-	-	2 (3.64)	15853 (.68)	2 (3.03)	18411 (.62)	- -	- -	1 (3.03)	2577 (.16)
10001-20000	7 (29.17)	106204 (14.80)	6 (10.91)	985596 (4.22)	11 (16.67)	180685 (6.04)	12 (23.53)	203929 (9.79)	3 (9.09)	47644 (2.97)
20001-30000	6 (25.0)	155110 (21.64)	15 (27.27)	376033 (16.08)	15 (22.73)	370833 (12.39)	13 (25.49)	319164 (15.32)	5 (15.15)	119128 (7.42)
30001-40000	8 (33.33)	273056 (38.10)	10 (18.18)	346916 (14.83)	11 (16.67)	380786 (12.72)	10 (19.61)	349929 (16.79)	6 (18.18)	214684 (13.36)
40001-50000	1 (4.17)	44745 (6.24)	6 (10.91)	271407 (11.60)	12 (18.18)	535169 (17.89)	6 (11.76)	270543 (12.98)	5 (15.16)	220997 (13.76)
50001-60000	1 (4.16)	58370 (8.14)	7 (12.73)	372904 (15.94)	4 (6.06)	226384 (7.56)	20 (3.92)	113450 (5.44)	3 (3.09)	163255 (10.16)
60001-70000	-	-	1 (1.82)	66350 (2.84)	3 (4.54)	195774 (6.54)	2 (3.92)	132271 (6.35)	3 (9.09)	185960 (11.58)
70001-80000	1 (4.17)	79386 (11.08)	2 (3.63)	154099 (6.59)	1 (1.57)	75796 (2.53)	-	-	2 (6.06)	148470 (9.24)
80001-90000	-	-	3 (5.45)	256069 (10.95)	2 (3.03)	164380 (5.49)	2 (3.92)	167947 (8.06)	2 (6.06)	169390 (10.54)
90001-Above	-	-	3 (5.46)	380616 (16.27)	5 (7.58)	844409 (28.22)	4 (7.85)	526433 (25.27)	3 (9.09)	334455 (20.82)
All Income Levels	24 (100.00)	716771 (100.00)	55 (100.00)	2338843 (100.00)	66 (100.00)	2992627 (100.00)	51 (100.00)	2083666 (100.00)	33 (100.00)	1606560 (100.00)
Average Income		29865.46		42524.42		45342.83		40865.19		48683.63
Average Income*				38678.65				43387.11		

(Contined)

Table 2.5 (i)

Distribution of Cultivator Households by income level and age of the Chief Earner

Income Level (In Rs.)	Age between 46-50 years		Age between 51-55 years		Age between 56 & Above		All farmers	
	Number	Amount	Number	Amount	Number	Amount	Number	Amount
upto-10000	-	-	-	-	-	-	5 (1.56)	36841 (1.25)
10001-20000	5 (14.29)	78932 (4.77)	1 (4.76)	15856 (1.36)	4 (11.43)	62291 (3.36)	49 (15.31)	794037 (5.50)
20001-30000	5 (14.29)	127602 (7.71)	4 (19.05)	92857 (7.96)	9 (25.71)	221752 (11.96)	72 (22.50)	782479 (12.33)
30001-40000	9 (25.71)	299167 (18.08)	2 (9.52)	64364 (5.51)	5 (14.29)	173735 (9.37)	61 (19.06)	2102637 (14.59)
40001-50000	5 (14.29)	226992 (13.72)	4 (19.05)	178618 (15.31)	-	-	39 (12.19)	1748471 (12.13)
50001-60000	3 (8.57)	163006 (9.85)	2 (9.53)	110031 (9.43)	6 (17.14)	317864 (17.15)	28 (8.75)	1525264 (10.58)
60001-70000	2 (5.71)	128788 (7.89)	1 (4.76)	62423 (5.35)	3 (8.57)	193825 (10.46)	15 (4.69)	965391 (6.70)
70001-80000	2 (5.71)	146347 (8.85)	2 (9.52)	153366 (13.14)	2 (5.71)	148889 (8.03)	12 (3.75)	906353 (6.29)
80001-90000	2 (5.71)	172322 (10.42)	2 (9.52)	175130 (15.00)	2 (5.72)	164390 (8.87)	15 (4.69)	1269628 (8.81)
90001-Above	2 (5.72)	311103 (18.81)	3 (14.29)	314404 (26.94)	4 (11.43)	570979 (30.80)	24 (7.50)	3282399 (22.77)
All Income Levels	35 (100.00)	1654259 (100.00)	21 (100.00)	1167049 (100.00)	35 (100.00)	1853725 (100.00)	320 (100.00)	14413500 (100.00)
Average Income		47264.54		55573.76		52963.57		45042.18
Average Incoome*		47953.22				53942.39		

Note : Figures in parentheses indicate the percentages.

* Computed on the basis of 10 years age-group.

ever, in the present study it is the age of the chief earner which has been taken into consideration. Accordingly, households have been classified into eight groups on the basis of the age of the chief earner in each household and the resulting picture is presented in Table 2.5 (i). Since the 5 year age-groups do not show any definite trend, we have also computed the 10 year age groups consisting of (i) upto 30 years (ii) 31 to 40 years, (iii) 41 to 50 years, and (iv) above 50 years which shows that there is positive increasing relationship between age of the chief earner and the average income. The results indicate that as the age of the chief earner rises, the average income of the households also tend to increase. In other words, average household income has been found to be relatively lower in the case of the chief earner being in the young age of upto 30 years as compared to the chief earner being in the old age-groups. It is reasonable to think that age and hence experience on job is a significant determine of differences in income. For example, a farmer gets maturity and experience as his age increases, which helps in increasing his income.

Table 2.5 (ii) shows the income inequality by age of the chief earner. As is evident from the table income inequality is maximum in the age group of 36-40 years and minimum in the age group of upto 25 years. However, Theil Index gives different results of income inequalities.

Education of the Chief Earner

The sample households have been classified on the basis of the level of education of the chief earner into five categories, vis.,

(i) No formal education, or illiterate,

(ii) Primary Level Education

(iii) Middle Level Education

(iv) Matric/Higher Secondary Level Education

Table 2.5 (ii)
Indicators of Income Inequality by Age of the Chief Earner

Inequality Indicators	Upto 25 years	26-30 years	31-35 years	36-40 years	41-45 years	46-50 years	51-56 years	56 Years and above
1. Concentration Ratio	.128	.201	.187	.297	.218	.156	.254	.179
2. Share of bottom Quintile (%)	13.46	11.43	12.19	9.65	9.94	12.95	9.09	12.68
Share of Top Quintile (%)	25.96	31.49	30.42	40.52	31.76	28.73	33.78	29.96
3. Coefficient of Variation of Income (%)	6.17	7.03	7.01	9.54	8.16	6.37	8.23	6.59
4. Standard Deviation of Logarithms of Income	-	.290	.280	.452	.327	.258	.345	.270
5. Theil Index	.124	.116	.117	.115	.147	.113	.122	.130

(v) Graduate/Postgraduate level education

It may be noted that the groupings are not as refined as they could possibly be. However, they are adequate for the present purpose. An inspection of the average income of the different household groups as shown in Table 2.6 (i) reveals that education of the chief earner in a family plays a positive role in raising the household income. Generally speaking, the households where the chief earners have had more years of schooling are also the households which are relatively better off economically. And this is more true of the households whose chief earners have graduate/post-graduate level of education. Another interesting aspect of the information generated by the table is the role of education in changing the income distribution pattern. The income distribution in the case of the households with school level education (of the chief earner) in terms of quintile shares and concentration ratios, have been found to be near equitable, except of course, with no formal education, as compared with the households whose chief earners have graduate/post-graduate level education. Since access to education of an individual does, to a large extent itself depend on the position of his family on the income scale, education can equally well be said to be a mechanism of reinforcing a given pattern of income distribution. More intensive and extensive analysis is in fact required to generate any really meaningful conclusions.

Size of the Cultivator Household

The sample households have been grouped into four different family sizes. A family upto 5 members has been viewed as of the smallest size and that with more than 9 members as of the largest size. In between are the other two size groups of families having 6-7 and 8-9 members. Table 2.7 (i) presents the income distribution for families according to size groups. It can be seen that the average cultivator household income tends to increase with the

Table 2.6 (i)
Distribution of Cultivator Households by the Levels of Income and Education

Income Level (in Rs.)	Not Formal Education		Primary		Middle		Matric		Graduate		Total	
	No. of House holds	Amount	No. of House holds	Amount	No. of House holds	Amount	No. of House holds	Amount	No. of House holds	Amount	No. of House holds	Amount
0-10000	4 (1.99)	28332 (.34)	-	-	-	-	1 (2.27)	8509 (.42)	-	-	5 (1.56)	36841 (1.25)
10001-20000	32 (15.92)	519432 (6.17)	3 (9.09)	48144 (3.04)	3 (9.37)	47935 (3.09)	10 (22.73)	164951 (8.12)	1 (10)	13565 (1.64)	49 (15.31)	794037 (5.50)
20001-30000	48 (23.88)	1202180 (14.28)	7 (21.21)	163765 (10.34)	7 (21.88)	177952 (11.45)	9 (20.45)	218332 (10.75)	1 (10)	20250 (2.45)	72 (22.50)	1782479 (12.33)
30001-40000	37 (18.41)	1272901 (15.12)	7 (21.22)	243602 (15.38)	6 (18.75)	209041 (13.45)	9 (20.45)	316336 (15.58)	2 (20)	60757 (7.35)	61 (19.06)	2102637 (14.59)
40001-50000	23 (10.44)	1029433 (12.23)	6 (18.18)	280789 (17.72)	6 (18.75)	263717 (16.97)	3 (6.82)	126488 (6.23)	1 (10)	48044 (5.81)	39 (12.19)	1748471 (12.13)
50001-60000	18 (8.96)	983085 (11.68)	4 (12.12)	216597 (13.67)	2 (6.25)	110022 (7.08)	3 (6.82)	1555756 (7.67)	1 (10)	59804 (7.23)	28 (8.75)	1525264 (10.58)
60001-70000	10 (4.98)	644015 (7.65)	-	-	2 (6.25)	131621 (8.47)	3 (6.82)	289755 (9.34)	-	-	15 (4.69)	965391 (6.70)
70001-80000	9 (4.47)	674440 (8.01)	1 (3.03)	79135 (4.99)	2 (6.25)	152778 (9.83)	-	-	-	-	12 (3.75)	906353 (6.29)
80001-90000	9 (4.48)	758050 (9.00)	2 (6.06)	164380 (20.38)	2 (6.25)	177484 (11.42)	2 (4.55)	169714 (8.36)	-	-	15 (4.69)	1269628 (8.81)
90001-Above	11 (5.47)	130610 (15.52)	3 (9.09)	387724 (24.48)	2 (6.25)	283362 (18.24)	4 (9.09)	680891 (33.53)	4 (10)	624321 (75.52)	24 (7.50)	3282399 (22.77)
All Income Levels	201	8417969	33	1584136	32	1553912	44	2030742	10	826741	320 (100,00)	14413500 (100.00)
Average Income		41880.44		48004.12		48559.75		46153.23		82674.10		45042.18

Note : Figures in parenthises denote percentages.

Table 2.6 (ii)
Indicators of Income Inequality by Education

Inequality Indicators	No formal Education	Primary	Middle	Matric	Graduate/ PG
1. Concentration Ratio	.308	.190	.216	.193	.427
2. Share of bottom Quintile (%)	7.93	11.95	11.26	12.36	4.09
Share of top Quintile (%)	39.84	30.72	33.37	32.08	44.76
3. Co-efficient of Variation of Income (%)	11.04	7.13	9.76	8.52	12.95
4. Standard Deviation of Logarithms of Income	.350	.274	.343	.281	.359
5. Theil Index	.118	.124	.114	.130	.234

size of family. This evidence lends credence to the view that the family size as an income-propelling force may operate both through the intensification of the efforts of the chief earner in the family and through the provision of supplementary earners[6].

Another interesting fact brought out by the table is that, relatively speaking, income is more evenly distributed among households, with a family size of 6-7 members, while it is relatively more unevenly distributed in households with 8-9 members. Income distribution tends to be more equitable in the case of households which are neither too small nor too large. The estimated values of concentration ratio, and quintile shares support this conclusion, namely, that there is no definitive relation between family size and equality of income distribution. This would seem to be so mainly because of the fact that family size alone is not a definitive, or even a major, casual variable in the household income generation process

Number of Earners

Almost by definition, the number of earners in a family would seem to be a significant determinant of its income level. We have, therefore, grouped the sample

Table 2.7 (i)
Distribution of Cultivator Households by Income Level and Family-size

Income Level	Upto 5 5 members		With 6-7 members		With 8-9 members		With more than 9 members		Total	
	Number	Amount	Number	Amount	Number	Amount	Number	Amount	Number	Amount
0-10000	4 (3.28)	26939 (.72)	1 (1.19)	9902 (.29)	-	-	-	-	5 (1.56)	368410 (1.25)
10001-20000	33 (27.05)	533576 (14.36)	9 (10.72)	147237 (4.30)	3 (7.50)	48696 (2.36)	4 (5.41)	64528 (1.24)	49 (15.31)	368410 (5.50)
20001-30000	35 (28.69)	871669 (23.46)	26 (30.95)	630038 (18.38)	6 (15.00)	146100 (7.09)	5 (6.76)	134672 (2.58)	72 (22.50)	1782479 (12.33)
30001-40000	22 (18.03)	757003 (20.37)	21 (25.00)	728616 (21.26)	11 (27.50)	365779 (17.75)	7 (9.46)	251239 (4.83)	61 (19.06)	2102637 (14.59)
40001-50000	14 (11.48)	621915 (16.74)	12 (14.29)	543756 (15.86)	5 (12.50)	225501 (10.94)	8 (10.81)	357299 (6.86)	39 (12.19)	1748471 (12.13)
50001-60000	8 (6.16)	444602 (11.96)	4 (4.76)	213910 (6.24)	6 (15.00)	313911 (15.23)	10 (13.51)	552841 (10.61)	28 (8.75)	1524264 (10.58)
60001-70000	2 (1.64)	133335 (3.59)	4 (4.76)	258176 (7.53)	1 (2.50)	62423 (3.03)	8 (10.81)	511457 (9.82)	15 (4.69)	965391 (6.70)
70001-80000	2 (1.63)	150699 (4.05)	2 (2.38)	148984 (4.35)	2 (5.00)	154350 (7.49)	6 (8.11)	452320 (8.68)	12 (3.75)	906353 (6.29)
80001-90000	1 (.82)	82910 2.23)	1 (1.19)	82325 (2.40)	1 (2.50)	83120 (4.04)	12 (16.21)	1021273 (19.61)	15 (4.69)	1269628 (8.81)
90001-Above	1 (.82)	93445 (2.51)	4 (4.76)	664594 (19.39)	5 (12.50)	660788 (32.07)	14 (18.92)	1863572 (35.77)	24 (7.50)	3282399 (22.77)
All Income Levels	122 (100.00)	3716093 (100.00)	84 (100.00)	3427538 (100.00)	40 (100.00)	2060668 (100.00)	74 (100.00)	5209201 (100.00)	320 (100.00)	14413500 (100.00)
Average Income		30459.78		408004.02		5156.70		70394.61		45042.18

Note : Figures in parentheses denote percentages.

Table 2.7 (ii)
Indicators of Income Inequality by Size of Family

Inequality Indicators	Upto 5 members	6-7 members	8-9 members	More than 9 members
1. Concentration Ratio	.252	.191	.333	.217
2. Share of bottom Quintile (%)	9.54	12.23	8.12	10.01
Share of top Quintile (%)	35.11	31.44	43.59	31.40
3. Co-efficient of Variation of Income (%)	10.21	9.52	12.03	10.14
4. Standard Deviation of Logarithms of Income.	.434	.259	.475	.334
5. Theil Index	.105	.111	.118	.131

households into five categories on the basis of the number of earners in the family to find out the nature and extent of the relation between the number of earners and the family income. Tables 2.8 (i) and 2.8 (ii) present the results. It is evident from the table that, on the one extreme, 11.56 per cent of the total cultivator households constitute single-earner households, while, on the other extreme, 14.38 per cent of the total households have 5 or more earners. Households with 2 to 4 earners constitute the bulk, i.e.74.06 per cent, of the total households. Two major implications flow from the Table : (i) The greater the number of earners in a family, the greater its income, excepting the family with 5 and more earners; (ii) The income distribution tends to be more equitable in the case of household groups at the two extremes, that is, the family consisting of only one earning member and the family consisting of five or more earning members.

It may, of course, be noted here that while the size of the family alone is too inadequate to explain its income levels, the number of earning members too is not by itself adequate in this context. Additional information as to the average quantum of the contribution of each earner is imperative in this respect.

Table 2.8 (i)
Distribution of Cultivator Households by Income Level and Number of Earners

Income Level	With 1 earner		With 2 earner		With 3 earner		With 4 earner		With 5 and more earners		Total	
	Number	Amount	Number	Amount	Number	Amount	Number	Amount	Number	Amount	Number	Amount
0-10000	3 (8.11)	18430 (1.56)	2 (1.49)	18411 (.42)	-	-	-	-	-	-	5 (1.56)	36841 (1.25)
10001-20000	8 (21.62)	126996 (10.72)	31 (23.13)	508654 (11.44)	6 (9.84)	92341 (3.01)	3 (7.14)	48842 (1.78)	2 (2.17)	17204 (.58)	49 (15.31)	794037 (5.50)
20001-30000	11 (29.73)	276478 (2.33)	37 (27.61)	894904 (20.13)	12 (19.67)	302848 (9.87)	6 (14.29)	149742 (5.45)	6 (13.04)	158507 (5.34)	72 (22.50)	1782479 (12.33)
30001-40000	5 (13.51)	175851 (14.85)	33 (24.63)	1134651 (25.52)	6 (9.84)	207288 (6.76)	7 (16.67)	243042 (8.85)	10 (21.74)	341805 (11.51)	61 (19.06)	2102637 (14.59)
40001-50000	3 (8.11)	125365 (10.58)	12 (8.96)	547261 (12.31)	11 (18.03)	495715 (16.16)	9 (21.43)	405921 (14.78)	4 (8.70)	174209 (5.87)	39 (12.19)	1748471 (12.13)
50001-60000	4 (10.81)	218014 (18.41)	10 (7.46)	559811 (12.59)	9 (14.75)	473071 (15.42)	2 (4.76)	113620 (4.14)	3 (6.52)	160748 (5.41)	28 (8.75)	1525264 (10.58)
60001-70000	1 (2.70)	67000 (5.66)	3 (2.24)	193921 (4.26)	4 (6.56)	251356 (8.20)	2 (4.76)	131172 (4.78)	5 (10.87)	321942 (10.84)	15 (4.69)	965391 (6.70)
70001-80000	-	-	-	-	7 (11.48)	529836 (17.27)	2 (4.76)	153366 (5.58)	3 (6.52)	223151 (7.52)	12 (3.75)	906353 (6.29)
80001-90000	1 (2.71)	82910 (7.00)	2 (1.49)	164125 (3.69)	2 (3.28)	173319 (5.65)	3 (7.14)	248419 (9.04)	7 (15.22)	600855 (30.24)	15 (4.69)	1269628 (8.81)
90001-Above	1 (2.70)	93445 (7.89)	4 (2.99)	424048 (9.54)	4 (6.55)	541777 (17.66)	8 (19.05)	1252477 (45.60)	7 (15.22)	970652 (32.69)	24 (7.50)	3282399 (22.77)
All Income (100.00)	37 (100.00)	1184489 (100.00)	134 (100.00)	4445786 (100.00)	61 (100.00)	3067551 (100.00)	42 (100.00)	2746601 (100.00)	46 (100.00)	2969073 (100.00)	320 (100.00)	14413500
Average Income	32013.22			33177.51		50287.72		65395.26		64545.06		45042.18

Note : Figures in parentheses denote percentages.

Table 2.8 (ii)
Indicators of Income-Inequality by Number of Earners

Inequality Indicators	With 1 earner	2 earners	3 earners	4 earners	5 & Above
1. Concentration Ratio	.147	.229	.263	.260	.172
2. Share of bottom Quintile (%)	12.92	10.74	8.80	9.99	12.90
Share of top Quintile (%)	27.91	33.94	35.42	36.34	29.24
3. Co-efficient of variation of Income	6.29	8.12	8.59	8.28	6.47
4. Standard Deviation of Logarithms of Income	.261	.278	.358	.325	.272
5. Theil Index	.119	.114	.116	.128	.127

Section II

In this section, we shall examine in detail the existing pattern of asset holdings among different categories of cultivator households. Economic inequality has been measured mainly with regard to assests, i.e., inequality in the distribution of assets. We shall also examine the role of socio-economic factors which determine the demand for a particular asset.

The role of assets as determinant of household saving has been widely recognised in recent approaches to consumption function, for instance, Friedman (1957), Modigliani (1963), Spiro (1962) and Clower and Johnson (1968). The volume and the character of the assets which the households possess at any point in time is likely to condition their desire to accumulate more.

As pointed out earlier, in Chapter One, in the present study, the assets have been defined to include all items owned by households which have money value and these have been divided into two parts : (i) physical and (ii) financial assets.

Physical assets include: land (including vacant house sites) buildings (residential and other property), cattle-sheds, farm buildings, live-stock, agricultural implements and machinery (including means of irrigation), business assets (including business premises, means of transport and other non-farm machinery) and consumer durables. Financial assets consist of the amount deposited with the banks / post offices, premia paid to the Life Insurance Corporation, provident fund contributions, shares and securities (of cooperative banks / societies and cooperative mills, etc.) and gold and jewellery. So far as the valuation of these assets is concerned, it is mainly based on the information supplied by the respondents during the reference period.

Asset-Structure

The asset-structure of the households in terms of percentage shares of different assets is presented in Table 2.9. It may be seen that for all cultivator households taken together, land dominates the total assets with a share of 78.46 per cent. Next in importance are buildings with a share of 7.58 per cent, followed by agricultural implements and machinery, and livestock with a share of 4.74 per cent and 3.09 per cent, respectively. The other assets account for a very small fraction of the total. Significantly, of the total assets, the physical assets alone account for 97.08 per cent whereas the financial assets account for only 2.92 per cent. The reason for this would seem to be that the financial assets are acquired and retained mainly as provision for the rainy days; these are available, or meant to be used, as working capital very exceptionly, if at all. Most of the needs for working capital are met from current borrowings. Financial assets, held mainly in the form of precious metals, are sometimes used as security for loans. These may, therefore, be considered a potential source, though a limited one, to be drawn upon for investment. Even if we leave a margin for underestimation and concealment,

Table 2.9
Volume and Composition of Assets of Cultivators Households
(Amount in Rs.)

Source	Large Farmers	Medium Farmers	Small Farmers	All Farmers
1. Land including House sites	81330000 (81.68)	33910000 (78.63)	34945000 (71.71)	150185000 (78.46)
2. Building residential only	5390000 (5.41)	3213000 (7.45)	5910500 (12.13)	14513500 (7.58)
3. Cattle sheds	835000 (0.84)	596600 (1.38)	1094100 (2.25)	2525700 (1.32)
4. Farm Buildings	1003500 (1.01)	406000 (0.94)	356700 (0.73)	1766200 (0.92)
5. Live-stock	2090450 (2.10)	1434500 (3.33)	2396650 (4.92)	5921600 (3.09)
6. Implements and Machinery	5203190 (5.23)	1917930 (4.45)	1952475 (4.01)	9073595 (4.74)
7. Consumer Durables	893160 (0.90)	349465 (0.81)	606470 (1.24)	1849095 (0.97)
8. Financial Assets	2821640 (2.83)	1299992 (3.01)	1465974 (3.01)	5587607 (2.92)
All Sources	99566940 (100.00)	43127487 (100.00)	48727869 (100.00)	191422296 (100.00)

Note: Figures in parentheses indicate percentages.

is allowed, it would be of little significance.

The asset structure varies across the three categories of cultivator households. For example, land dominates the total assets in the case of large farmers with a share of 81.68 per cent, while the percentage share of this asset is 78.63 and 71.71 per cent in the case of medium and small farmers, respectively. . Among the large and medium farmers buildings, and implements and machinery are the other assets accounting for 5.41, 5.23 per cent and 7.45, 4.45 per cent, respectively.

Buildings, livestock, and implements and machinery occupy 12.13 per cent, 4.92 per cent and 4.01 per cent shares, respectively, among the small farmers. Whereas financial assets occupy fourth position in the case of large farmers accounting for 2.83 per cent, in the case of medium and small farmers it comes at fifth position accounting for 3.01 per cent for both the categories.

To some extent, the differential in the asset structrure of different categories of cultivator households could perhaps be narrowed down if the level of education, availability of the irrigation and, importantly, financial facilities, etc., were brought into the picture as explanatory variables. Admittedly, for a comprehensive analysis of the asset-sturcture of the households, some sort of homogeneous grouping of the households is essential. One could adopt various possible criteria for one's classifcatory scheme, e.g., location, total asset-position, etc. Our own adoption of the size of land holding as the criterion has a positive and definitive edge, or rationale, in its favour, for, gross income flowing from and the requirement of productive assets (such as implements and machinary) are more or less the same for cultivators with the same size of land holding.

Distribution of Assets

For examining the distribution of assets, we have grouped the cultivators in each size category by the level of asset holding. In all, thirteen asset levels have been conceived, but for the purpose of analysis assets less than worth Rs. 5,00,000 have been taken as constituting the lowest asset level and asset valuing more than Rs. 20,00,000 constituting the highest asset level. The pattern of asset distribution emerging from this grouping is presented in Table 2.10. In the case of large farmers only 2.82 per cent of the cultivator households in this category fall in the lower asset class upto Rs. 5,00, 000 and they account for only 0.71 per cent to the total assets. 21.13 per cent, the maximum proportion in this category,

Table 2.10 Distribution of Cultivator Households by the Level of Assets

Asset Level	Large Farmers		Medium Farmers		Small Farmers		Total Farmers	
	Number	Amount	Number	Amount	Number	Amount	Number	Amount
Upto - 1,00,000	-	-	-	-	11 (6.01)	920410 (1.89)	11 (3.44)	920410 (.48)
100001-2,00,000	-	-	-	-	50 (27.32)	8180660 (16.79)	50 (15.63)	8180660 (4.27)
200001-3,00,000	1 (1.41)	207550 (0.21)	-	-	75 (40.99)	18420424 (37.80)	76 (23.75)	18627974 (9.73)
3,00,001-4,00,000	-	-	6 (9.09)	2072870 (4.81)	30 (16.40)	10121475 (20.77)	36 (11.25)	12194345 (6.37)
4,00,001-5,00,000	1 (1.41)	496155 (0.50)	18 (27.27)	7975575 (18.49)	5 (2.73)	2184210 (4.48)	24 (7.50)	10655940 (5.57)
5,00,001-6,00,000	-	-	19 (28.79)	10431180 (24.19)	3 (1.64)	1654530 (3.40)	22 (6.88)	12085710 (6.31)
6,00,001-7,00,000	4 (5.63)	2576840 (2.59)	8 (12.12)	5088187 (11.80)	2 (1.09)	1296300 (2.66)	14 (4.37)	8961327 (4.68)
7,00,001-8,00,000	13 (18.31)	9715215 (9.76)	5 (7.58)	3718685 (8.62)	3 (1.64)	2191700 (4.50)	21 (6.56)	15625600 (8.16)
8,00,001-9,00,000	9 (12.68)	7723475 (7.76)	-	-	2 (1.09)	1727600 (3.54)	11 (3.44)	9451075 (4.94)
,090,001-10,00,000	8 (11.27)	7671005 (7.70)	-	-	-	-	8 (2.50)	7671005 (4.01)
1000001-1500000	15 (21.13)	18016565 (18.09)	8 (12.11)	10076490 (23.36)	2 (1.09)	2030560 (4.17)	25 (7.81)	30123615 (15.74)
1500001-2000000	10 (14.08)	17440630 (17.52)	1 (1.52)	1611600 (3.74)	-	-	11 (3.43)	19052230 (9.95)
2000001-Above	10 (14.08)	35719505 (35.87)	1 (1.52)	2152900 (4.99)	-	-	11 (3.44)	37872405 (19.79)
All Asset Levels	71 (100.00)	99566940 (100.00)	66 (100.00)	43127487 (100.00)	183 (100.00)	48727869 (100.00)	320 (100.00)	191422296 (100.00

Note : Figures in parentheses denote percentages.)

falls in the Rs. 10,00,001-15,00,000 asset group and accounts for 18.09 per cent of the total assets. 14.08 per cent households in this size category fall in the highest asset group and account for a 35.87 per cent share of the total assets held by the category as a whole.

Among the medium farmers, 36.36 per cent households fall in the lowest asset group (upto Rs. 500000) with a 23.3 per cent share in the total assets of the category. 28.79 per cent households, the highest fall in the Rs. 500001 - 600000 asset group, accounting for 24.19 per cent of the total assets, and only 1.52 per cent households in this category fall in the highest asset group with a 4.99 per cent share in the total assets.

In the case of small farmers, 93.45 per cent households, the highest proportion in any size category, fall in the lowest asset-group and account for the bulk, i.e., 81.73 per cent, of the total assets of this category. Interestingly, but not unexpectedly, not even a single farmer in this category falls in the highest asset group.

For all households taken together, 61.57 per cent fall in the lower asset group, accounting for 26.42 per cent of the total assets, while 3.44 per cent households fall in the highest asset group, accounting for 19.79 per cent of total assets.

The average value of asset holding of the large farmers is greater as compared to that of the medium and small farmers, being Rs. 14,02,351.30, Rs. 6,53,446.77 and Rs. 2,66,272.51, respectively. And on the whole, the average value of the asset holdings is Rs. 5,98,194.67.

A more informative, and analytically more meaningful, distribution of assets emerges if the households are distributed by decile. It can be seen from Table 2.11 that the top 10 per cent of the cultivator households in rural Haryana hold about 37 per cent, i.e., about two fifths, of the total assets, while the bottom 10 per cent hold a mere 2 per cent. Category-wise the shares of the top 10 per cent

Table 2.11
Distribution of Cultivator Households by Deciles

Decile Group	Large Farmers		Medium Farmers		Small Farmers		All Farmers	
	Percentage shares in total asset	Cumulative Percentage	Percentage shares in total asset	Cumulative Percentage	Percentage shares in total asset	Cumulative Percentage	Percentage shares in total asset	Cumulative Percentage
1st Decile	4.56	4.56	6.97	6.97	4.23	4.23	2.01	2.01
2nd Decile	5.69	10.25	7.83	14.80	6.20	10.43	3.06	5.07
3rd Decile	6.11	16.36	8.24	23.04	7.22	17.65	3.75	8.82
4th Decile	6.65	23.01	8.92	31.96	8.17	25.82	4.30	13.12
5th Decile	7.26	30.27	9.42	41.38	8.97	34.79	5.19	18.31
6th Decile	7.96	38.23	9.80	51.18	9.54	44.33	6.82	25.13
7th Decile	9.37	47.60	10.09	61.27	10.39	54.72	9.21	34.34
8th Decile	11.46	59.06	10.75	72.02	11.55	66.27	12.10	46.44
9th Decile	14.71	73.77	11.76	83.78	13.11	79.38	16.66	63.10
10th Decile	26.23	100.00	16.22	100.00	20.62	100.00	36.90	100.00

is about 26 per cent in the case of the large farmers, 16 per cent in the case of medium farmers, and 21 per cent in the case of small farmers. In contrast, the shares of the bottom 10 per cent in the three size categories are only 4.56 per cent, 6.97 per cent and 4.23 per cent, respectively. The relative position of the top 20 per cent of the large farmers on the asset scale is superior to their counterparts in the other size categories. But the bottom 80 per cent of the large farmers are worse off as compared to the bottom 80 per cent in the other categories in this respect. The above pattern is confirmed when concentration ratio, co-efficient of variation, and standard deviation of logarithms are computed (Table 2.12).

Table 2.12
Indicators of Asset Inequality by Category of Cultivator Households of Farmers

Inequality Indicators	Large Farmers	Medium Farmers	Small Farmers	All Farmers
1. Concentration Ratio	.294	.127	.225	.467
2. Share of bottom Quintile (%)	10.25	14.80	10.43	5.07
Share of top Quintile (%)	40.94	27.98	33.73	53.56
3. Coefficient variation of Assets	13.41	9.72	12.23	15.16
4. Standard Deviation of Logarithms of Asset	.448	.327	.414	.481
5. Theil Index	.142	.110	.096	.102

Our analysis thus brings out that wide disparities in terms of asset holdings characterize all the households taken together, in general, and the large households taken separately, in particular. The disparities as depicted from the table are also shown through Figures 2.5 to 2.8.

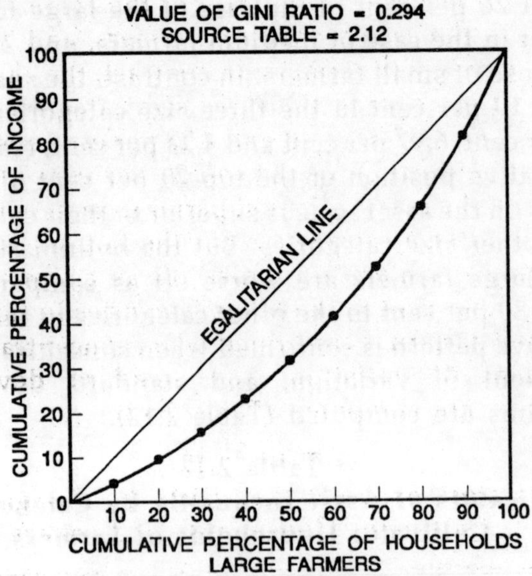

Fig. 2.5. Lorenz Curve Showing Asset Inequality

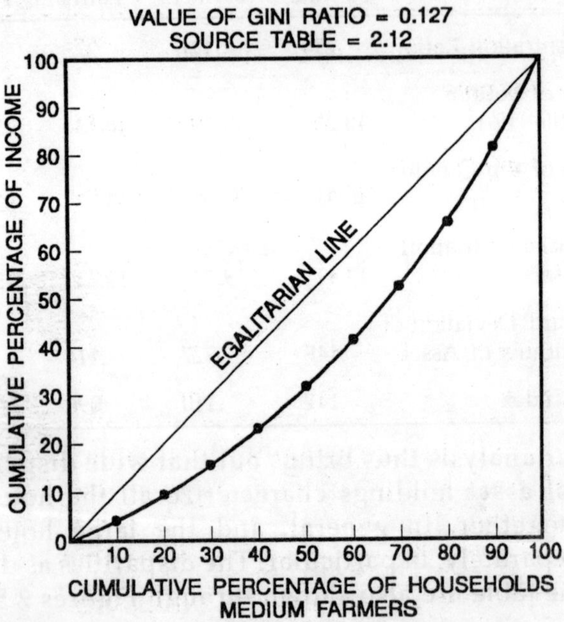

Fig. 2.6. Lorenz Curve Showing Asset Inequality

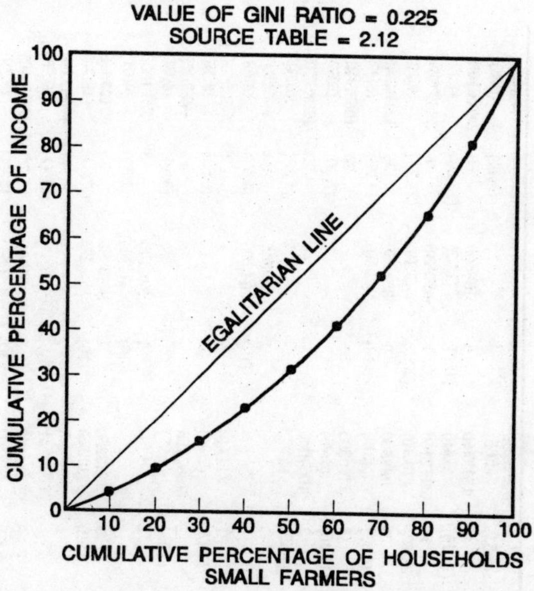

Fig. 2.7. Lorenz Curve Showing Asset Inequality

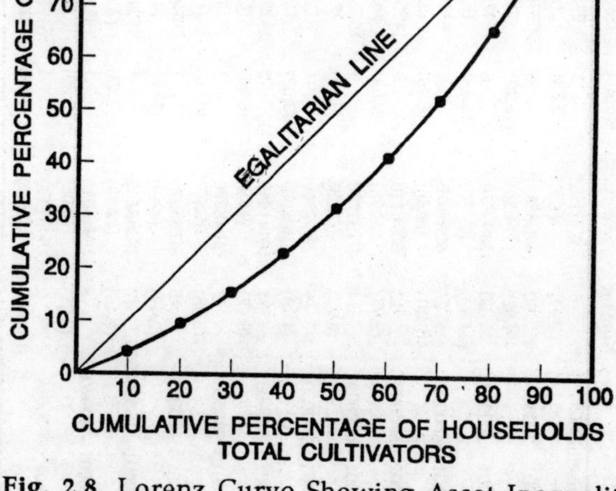

Fig. 2.8. Lorenz Curve Showing Asset Inequality

Table 2.13 (i)

Distribution of Cultivator Households by the Levels of Assets and Education

Asset Level (In Rs.)	No Formal Education		Primary		Middle		Matric		Graduate & Above		All Farmers	
	Number	Amount	Number	Amount	Number	Amount	Number	Amount	Number	Amount	Number	Amount
Upto - 100000	6 (2.99)	475350 (.45)	1 (3.03)	93320 (.41)	1 (3.12)	96490 (.44)	3 (6.81)	255250 (1.05)	-	-	11 (3.44)	920410 (0.48)
100001 - 200000	30 (14.92)	4796580 (4.50)	6 (18.18)	1029040 (4.47)	5 (15.63)	845680 (3.82)	8 (18.18)	1319760 (5.45)	1 (10.0)	189600 (1.22)	50 (15.63)	8180660 (4.27)
200001 - 300000	50 (24.87)	12499670 (11.72)	6 (18.18)	1507844 (6.54)	4 (12.50)	957450 (4.33)	14 (31.82)	3172160 (13.10)	2 (20.0)	490850 (3.18)	76 (23.75)	18627974 (9.73)
300001 - 400000	27 (13.43)	9239875 (8.66)	2 (6.06)	630920 (2.74)	3 (9.37)	980400 (4.43)	3 (6.82)	988500 (4.08)	1 (10)	354650 (2.30)	36 (11.25)	12194345 (6.37)
400001 - 500000	12 (5.97)	5278110 (4.95)	3 (9.09)	1455405 (6.32)	4 (12.50)	1756120 (7.95)	5 (11.36)	2166305 (8.95)	-	-	24 (7.50)	10655940 (5.57)
500001 - 600000	14 (6.97)	7731730 (7.25)	3 (9.09)	1653150 (7.18)	3 (9.37)	1636830 (7.41)	2 (4.55)	1064000	-	-	22 (6.88)	12085710 (6.31)
600001 - 700000	9 (4.48)	5697760 (5.34)	1 (3.03)	612780 (2.66)	3 (9.38)	2021487 (9.15)	-	-	1 (10)	629300 (4.08)	14 (4.37)	8961327 (4.68)
700001 - 800000	14 (6.97)	10441665 (9.79)	2 (6.06)	1425085 (6.19)	4 (12.50)	3047110 (13.79)	1 (2.27)	711740 (2.94)	-	-	21 (6.56)	15625600 (8.16)
800001 - 900000	7 (3.48)	6048270 (5.67)	2 (6.06)	1715650 (7.45)	-	-	2 (4.55)	1687155 (6.97)	-	-	11 (3.44)	9451075 (4.94)
900001 - 1000000	5 (2.49)	4785970 (4.49)	1 (3.03)	970600 (4.21)	1 (3.03)	970335 (4.39)	-	-	1 (10)	944100 (6.11)	8 (2.50)	7671005 (4.01)
1000001 - 15000000	17 (8.46)	20245665 (18.99)	4 (12.13)	4924850 (21.38)	-	-	3 (6.82)	3522250 (14.55)	1 (10)	1430850 (9.27)	25 (7.81)	30123615 (15.74)
1500001 - 2000000	8 (3.98)	13916010 (13.05)	1 (3.03)	1522970 (6.61)	2 (6.25)	3613250 (16.35)	-	-	-	-	11 (3.43)	19052230 (9.95)
Above 2000000	2 (1.49)	5481250 (5.14)	1 (3.03)	5492130 (23.84)	2 (6.25)	6175525 (27.94)	3 (6.82)	93222100 (38.51)	3 (30)	11401400 (73.84)	11 (3.44)	37872405 (19.79)
All Asset Levels	201 (100.00)	106637905 (100.00)	33 (100.00)	23033744 (100.00)	32 (100.00)	22100677 (100.00)	44 (100.00)	24209220 (100.00)	10 (100.00)	15440750 (100.00)	320 (100.00)	191422296 (100.00)
Average Asset		530536.84		697992.24		690646.16		550209.55		1544075		

Note: Figures in parantheses indicate percentages.

Level of Education

Education is an important social variable which shapes the general outlook of a man and his ability to manage and control productive resources. We shall now see how far the level of education has any bearing on the quantum of assets of the cultivator households in the State. An examination of Tables 2.13 (i) and (ii) show that education has failed to reduce the concentration of assets. The households, both with no formal education and with higher education are concentrated in the higher asset levels. In the case of the households falling between these two ends, i.e., the households with formal education and with middle education level, assets are evenly distributed. The same pattern is confirmed by the Gini ratio and other measures.

Table 2.13 (ii)
Indicators of Asset Inequality by Education

Inequality Indicators	Not formal Education	Primary Level	Middle	Matric	Graduate/PG
1. Concentration Ratio	.394	.230	.273	.203	.545
2. Share of bottom Quintile (%)	6.32	11.37	9.86	13.01	2.63
Share of top Quintile (%)	46.45	34.07	36.76	34.35	58.77
3. Coefficient of Variation of Asset (%)	13.69	10.73	12.91	9.45	14.23
4. Standard Deviation of Logarithms of Assets	.425	.419	.424	.405	.426
5. Theil Index	.099	.106	.122	.126	.198

Size of Family

The average asset holdings of cultivator households tend to rise with an increase in the family size of the house-hold. Four different family sizes have been considered. A family upto five members has been viewed as of the smallest size and that with more than 9 members as of the largest size. In between are families having 6-7 and 8-9 members. Table 2.14 (i) presents the asset distribution

Table 2.14 (i)
Distribution of Cultivator Households by the Levels of Assets and Family Size

Asset Level	Upto 5 members		With 6-7 members		With 8-9 members		With 9 & more members		Total	
	Number	Amount	Number	Amount	Number	Amount	Number	Amount	Number	Amount
0 - 100000	6	507000	2	159310	2	163000	1	91100	11	920410
	(4.92)	(1.05)	(2.38)	(0.37)	(5.00)	(0.56)	(1.35)	(0.13)	(3.44)	(0.48)
100001 - 200000	28	4540660	12	1961490	4	696560	6	981950	50	8180660
	(22.95)	(9.41)	(14.29)	(4.59)	(10.00)	(2.38)	(8.11)	(1.38)	(15.63)	(4.27)
200001 - 300000	36	8777064	24	5906400	8	1984980	8	1959530	75	18627974
	(29.50)	(18.18)	(28.57)	(1.38)	(20.00)	(6.79)	(10.81)	(2.75)	(23.75)	(9.73)
300001 - 400000	17	5618045	7	2506500	6	2017050	6	2052750	36	12194345
	(13.93)	(11.64)	(8.33)	(5.87)	(15.00)	(6.90)	(8.11)	(2.88)	(11.25)	(6.37)
400001 - 500000	5	2186530	14	6287735	3	1267025	2	914650	24	10655940
	(4.10)	(4.53)	(16.67)	(14.73)	(7.50)	(4.33)	(2.70)	(1.28)	(7.50)	(5.57)
500001 - 600000	10	5442065	7	3897945	-	-	5	2745700	22	12085710
	(8.20)	(11.27)	(8.33)	(9.13)			(6.76)	(3.85)	(6.86)	(6.31)
600001 - 700000	3	1902730	3	1917830	3	1979580	5	3161187	14	8961327
	(2.46)	(3.94)	(3.58)	(4.49)	(7.50)	(6.77)	(6.76)	(4.44)	(4.37)	(4.68)
700001 - 800000	8	6039470	3	2242205	2	1443050	8	5900875	21	15625600
	(6.56)	(12.51)	(3.57)	(5.25)	(5.00)	(4.94)	(10.81)	(8.28)	(6.56)	(8.16)
800001 - 900000	2	1676575	3	2593730	1	890850	5	4289920	11	9451075
	(1.64)	(3.47)	(3.57)	(6.07)	(0.25)	(3.05)	(6.75)	(6.02)	(3.44)	(4.94)
900001 - 1000000	2	1940650	2	1932370	2	1940935	2	1857050	8	7671005
	(1.64)	(4.02)	(2.38)	(4.52)	(5.00)	(6.64)	(2.70)	(2.61)	(2.50)	(4.01)
1000001 - 1500000	2	2412750	3	3613080	5	5574350	15	18523435	25	30123615
	(1.64)	(5.00)	(3.57)	(8.46)	(12.50)	(19.07)	(20.27)	(26.01)	(7.81)	(15.74)
1500001 - 2000000	1	1611600	3	4965770	1	1635000	6	10839860	11	19052230
	(0.82)	(3.34)	(3.57)	(11.63)	(0.25)	(5.59)	(8.11)	(15.21)	(3.43)	(9.95)
2000001 - Above	2	5618400	1	4701700	3	9643250	5	17909055	11	37872405
	(1.64)	(11.64)	(1.19)	(11.01)	(7.50)	(32.98)	(6.75)	(25.15)	(3.44)	(19.79)
All Asset Levels	122	48273539	84	42686065	40	29235630	74	71227062	320	191422296
	(100.00)	(100.00)	(100.00)	(100.00)	(100.00)	(100.00)	(100.00)	(100.00)	(100.00)	(100.00)
Average Asset		395684.75		508167.44		730890.75		96252786		

Note: Figures in parentheses denote percentages.

Table 2.14(ii)
Indicators of Asset Inequality by Family Size

Inequality Indicators	Upto 5 members	6-7 members	8-9 members	More than 9 members
1. Concentration Ratio	.312	.254	.489	.281
2. Share of bottom Quintile (%)	8.90	10.45	4.45	8.27
Share of top Quintile (%)	41.52	36.10	54.20	36.29
3. Coefficient of Variation of Assets (%)	13.84	11.83	15.29	12.68
4. Standard Deviation of Logarithms of Asset	.422	.412	.436	.421
5. Theil Index	.090	.097	.116	.117

Table 2.15(i)
Distribution of Cultivator Households by the Levels of Assets and Number of Earners

Asset Level	With 1 earner		With 2 earners		With 3 earners		With 4 earners		With 5 & more		Total	
	Number	Amount	Number	Amount	Number	Amount	Number	Amount	Number	Amount	Number	Amount
upto - 100000	4	323550	6	526310	1	70550	-	-	-	-	11	920410
	(10.81)	(1.81)	(4.48)	(1.03)	(1.64)	(.14)					(3.44)	(0.48)
100001 - 200000	6	931800	30	484650	7	1214950	3	458070	4	701190	50	8180600
	(16.22)	(5.21)	(22.39)	(9.59)	(11.47)	(2.46)	(7.14)	(1.36)	(8.70)	(1.77)	(15.63)	(4.27)
200001 - 300000	11	2618950	34	8130204	15	3763150	7	1882750	9	2232920	76	18627974
	(29.73)	(14.63)	(25.37)	(15.99)	(24.59)	(7.62)	(16.67)	(5.60)	(19.56)	(5.63)	(23.75)	(9.73)
300001 - 400000	4	1280500	20	6821945	4	1304250	6	2152450	2	635200	36	12194345
	(10.81)	(7.15)	(14.93)	(13.41)	(6.56)	(2.64)	(14.29)	(6.40)	(4.35)	(1.60)	(11.25)	(6.37)
400001 - 500000	3	1327450	12	5317760	5	2180530	1	470500	3	1359700	24	10655940
	(8.11)	(7.42)	(8.95)	(10.46)	(8.20)	(4.42)	(2.38)	(14.00)	(6.52)	(3.43)	(7.50)	(5.57)
500001 - 600000	2	1057580	11	6085450	2	1096050	4	2241180	3	1605450	22	12085710
	(5.41)	(5.91)	(8.21)	(11.97)	(3.28)	(2.22)	(9.52)	(6.67)	(6.52)	(4.09)	(6.88)	(6.31)
600001 - 700000	-	-	4	2587587	2	1351400	4	2512280	4	2510060	14	8961327
			(2.98)	(5.09)	(3.28)	(2.74)	(9.52)	(7.47)	(8.70)	(6.33)	(4.37)	(4.68)
700001 - 800000	2	1481100	5	3709485	3	2194550	4	3011920	7	5228545	21	15625600
	(5.41)	(8.28)	(3.73)	(7.29)	(4.92)	(4.44)	(9.53)	(8.96)	(15.22)	(13.18)	(6.56)	(8.16)
800001 - 900000	1	844500	5	4299225	2	1675030	1	890850	2	1741470	11	9451075
	(2.70)	(4.72)	(3.73)	(8.45)	(3.28)	(3.39)	(2.38)	(2.65)	(4.35)	(4.68)	(3.44)	(4.94)
900001 - 1000000	-	-	1	944100	2	1957920	3	2911935	2	1857050	8	7671005
			(.75)	(1.86)	(3.28)	(3.97)	(7.14)	(8.66)	(4.35)	(4.68)	(2.50)	(4.01)
1000001 - 1500000	2	2412750	5	592230	9	10978280	4	5178075	5	5632280	25	30123615
	(5.40)	(13.48)	(3.73)	(11.65)	(14.75)	(22.24)	(9.52)	(15.40)	(10.87)	(14.19)	(7.81)	(15.74)
1500001 - 2000000	-	-	1	1635000	6	10617500	3	4863380	1	1936350	11	19052230
			(.75)	(3.21)	(9.83)	(21.50)	(7.15)	(14.47)	(2.17)	(4.88)	(3.43)	(9.95)
2000001 - Above	2	5618400	-	-	3	10969200	2	7047425	4	14237380	11	37872405
	(2.70)	(31.39)			(4.92)	(22.22)	(4.76)	(2.96)	(8.69)	(35.88)	(3.44)	(19.79)
All Asset Levels	37	17896580	134	50853946	61	49373360	42	33620815	46	39677595	320	191422296
	(100.00)	(100.00)	(100.00)	(100.00)	(100.00)	(100.00)	(100.00)	(100.00)	(100.00)	(100.00)	(100.00)	(100.00)
Average Asset		483691.35		379507.06		809399.34		800495.60		862556.41		

Note: Figures in parentheses denote percentages.

for families of a given size. There is unequal distribution of assets in different family sizes. The value of concentration ratio decreases as we move from households with small families to households with having 6-7 family members, and increases for households with a family of 8-9 members and then decreases for households with largest family size, exhibiting an erratic behaviour. However, average asset shows a positive increasing trend with the family size. The assets are more unevently distributed among households with family of 8-9 members and evenly distributed among households with 6-7 members. The same pattern emerges from the coefficient of variation, and standard deviation of logarithms as presented in Table 2.14 (ii).

Number of Earners

The number of earners in a family is asignificant determinant of its assets. It is evident from Table 2.15(i) that the average value of assets owned by single-earner households is Rs. 4,83,691. It is lesser for the two earner households. However, it increases to Rs. 8,09,399 when we move to the three earners households. When households with five or more earners are considered, the amount is still higher, being Rs. 8,62,556. This behaviour/ pattern can be explained to a large extent by the fact that there is certain normally required ratio of tools per labourer so that a larger membership in a household results in possessing more tools and implements needed for work on the farms or in business or in other activity.

Assets are more evenly distributed in the case of the one earner families. They are evenly distributed among families with five and more earners as compared to all the other groups. The standard deviation of logarithms of income, shares of quintiles, coefficient of variations and concentration ratio confirm these results (Table 2.15 (ii).

Table 2.15(ii)
Indicators of Asset Inequality by Number of Earners

Inequality Indicators	With 1 earner	2 earner	3 earner	4 earner	5 & Above
1. Concentration Ratio	.114	.294	.405	.275	.165
2. Share of bottom Quintile (%)	14.92	9.03	6.35	9.41	12.98
Share of Quintile (%)	26.79	38.95	46.59	36.95	28.54
3. Coefficient of variation of Asset (%)	8.39	15.74	18.38	14.02	9.32
4. Standard Deviation of Logarithms	.349	.425	.429	.356	.353
5. Theil Index	.121	.094	.114	.106	.109

Age of Chief Earner

Table 2.16(i) shows that as we move from the households where chief earners are in the age group of upto 25 years to those in the 26-30 and 31-35 years age groups, the average value of assets tends to increase. However, it declines when we move to the next age group (36-40). In the age group of 56 years and above, the average value of assets is the highest compared to that with all other age-groups. The age of the chief earner does seem to have some role to play in building up the assets of the household.

The assets are more unevenly distributed among the households with chief earner in the middle age-groups 36-40 and 51-55 years, while the assets are evenly distributed among households with the young and old age-groups of upto 25 years and 56 years and above.

Table 2.16(i)
Distribution of Cultivator Households by the Levels of Assets and Age of Chief Earner

Asset Level (In Rs.)	Upto 25 years		Age between 26-30 years		Age between 31-35 years		Age between 36-40 years	
	Number	Amount	Number	Amount	Number	Amount	Number	Amount
Upto-100000	1 (4.17)	81750 (0.74)	3 (5.45)	230200 (.87)	-	-	2 (3.92)	175840 (.66)
100001-200000	5 (20.83)	890810 (8.05)	4 (7.27)	641790 (2.41)	15 (22.72)	2345660 (6.00)	10 (19.61)	1707590 (6.62)
200001-300000	5 (20.83)	1258240 (11.38)	18 (38.73)	4311910 (16.22)	14 (21.21)	3265470 (8.35)	18 (35.30)	4563694 (17.17)
300001-400000	4 (16.67)	1499600 (13.56)	9 (16.36)	3018275 (11.35)	6 (9.09)	2075900 (5.31)	2 (3.92)	633970 (2.34)
400001-500000	-	-	3 (5.45)	1282040 (4.82)	7 (10.60)	3200060 (8.18)	6 (11.77)	2603980 (9.80)
500001-600000	3 (12.50)	1677100 (15.17)	2 (3.64)	1063580 (4.00)	5 (7.58)	2762625 (7.06)	2 (3.92)	1037045 (3.90)
600001-700000	1 (4.17)	643800 (5.82)	1 (1.82)	699250 (2.63)	2 (3.03)	1214580 (3.10)	2 (3.92)	1314137 (4.95)
700001-800000	3 (12.50)	2278900 (20.61)	6 (10.91)	4479750 (16.85)	5 (7.58)	3655810 (9.34)	-	-
800001-900000	-	-	4 (7.27)	3409910 (12.83)	2 (3.03)	1728245 (4.42)	1 (1.96)	832800 (3.13)
900001-1000000	-	-	1 (1.82)	908300 (3.42)	3 (4.55)	2911250 (7.44)	2 (3.92)	1919085 (7.22)
1000001-1500000	1 (4.17)	1204800 (10.90)	2 (3.64)	2270550 (8.54)	4 (6.06)	4702750 (12.02)	3 (5.88)	3288350 (12.37)
1500001-2000000	1 (4.16)	1522970 (13.77)	1 (1.82)	1936350- (7.29)	-	-	-	
2000000-Above	-	-	1 (1.82)	2330350 (8.77)	3 (4.55)	11257700 (28.78)	3 (5.88)	8501925 (31.99)
All Asset Levels	24 (100.00)	11057870 (100.00)	55 (100.00)	26582255 (100.00)	66 (100.00)	39120050 (100.00)	51 (100.00)	26578416 (100.00)
Average Asset		460748.75		483313.73		592728.03		521145.41

(Continued)

Table 2.16(i)

Distribution of Cultivator Households by the Levels of Assets and Age of Chief Earner

Asset Level (In Rs.)	Upto 25 years		Age between 26-30 years		Age between 31-35 years		Age between 36-40 years	
	Number	Amount	Number	Amount	Number	Amount	Number	Amount
upto-100000	2	172260	11	93320	1	96490	1	70550
	(6.06)	(.77)	(2.86)	(.43)	(4.76)	(.76)	(2.86)	(.22)
100001-200000	7	1039750	2	379590	1	196650	6	978820
	(21.22)	(4.66)	(5.72)	(1.76)	(4.76)	(1.54)	(17.14)	(3.11)
200001-300000	3	776360	11	2717670	4	946350	3	788280
	(9.09)	(3.48)	(31.43)	(12.60)	(19.05)	(7.42)	(8.57)	(2.50)
300001-400000	2	608100	5	1574350	2	618500	6	2165650
	(6.06)	(2.72)	(14.29)	(7.30)	(9.52)	(4.85)	(17.14)	(6.89)
400001-500000	1	424730	2	859730	4	1865400	1	420000
	(3.03)	(1.90)	(5.71)	(3.99)	(19.05)	(14.63)	(2.86)	(1.34)
500001-600000	4	2144200	-	-	3	1681750	3	1719310
	(12.12)	(9.61)			(14.29)	(13.19)	(8.57)	(5.47)
600001-700000	1	655450	4	2532480	1	628180	2	1273450
	(3.03)	(2.94)	(11.43)	(11.74)	(4.76)	(4.93)	(5.71)	(4.05)
700001-800000	4	3011840	1	781500	-	-	2	1417800
	(12.12)	(13.49)	(2.86)	(3.62)			(5.71)	(4.51)
800001-900000	3	2615120	1	865000	-	-	-	-
	(9.09)	(11.71)	(2.86)	(4.01)				
900001-1000000	-	-	-	-	1	971000	1	961370
					(4.76)	(7.61)	(2.86)	(3.06)
1000001-1500000	2	2438490	4	4530320	3	4077550	6	7610805
	(6.06)	(10.92)	(11.42)	(21.01)	(14.29)	(31.97)	(17.14)	(24.21)
1500001-2000000	2	3135100	4	7232710	1	1670800	2	3554300
	(6.06)	(14.04)	(11.42)	(33.54)	(4.76)	(13.10)	(5.72)	(11.31)
2000001-Above	2	5303800	-	-	-	-	2	10478630
	(6.06)	(23.76)					(5.72)	(33.33)
All Asset Levels	33	22325300	35	21566670	21	12752670	35	31438965
	(100.00)	(100.00)	(100.00)	(100.00)	(100.00)	(100.00)	(100.00)	(100.00)
Average Asset		676524.24		616190.57		607270		898256.14

Note: Figures in parentheses denote percentages.

Table 2.16(ii)
Indicators of Asset Inequality by the Age of Chief Earner

Inequality Indicators	Upto 25 Years	26 - 30 Years	31 - 35 Years	36 - 40 Years	41 - 45 Years	46 - 50 Years	51 - 55 Years	56 Years and above
1. Concentration Ratio	.175	.232	.212	.366	.260	.202	.318	.193
2. Share of bottom Quintile (%)	13.10	11.29	12.13	8.51	9.45	13.09	8.31	12.58
3. Share of top Quintile (%)	30.32	35.28	33.06	48.13	35.57	35.59	42.21	32.49
4. Coefficient of Variation of Asset(%)	8.13	15.37	14.09	20.29	16.41	11.21	17.68	9.82
5. Standard Deviation of Logarithms of Asset	.353	.398	.384	.469	.403	.371	.409	.370
6. Theil Index	.128	.097	.104	.116	.115	.128	.127	.126

References

1. Goldsmith, I.R.W.; *A Study of Savings in the United States*, Vol. II, Princetion University Press, 1955, p. 47.

2. Nagar, A.L. and R.K. Dass; *Basic Statistics*, Oxford University Press, New Delhi, 1977, p. 380.

3. Klien, L.R., *An Introduction to Econometrics*, Prentice Hall of India (Pvt.) Ltd., New Delhi, 1965, p. 155.

4. Debroy, B., "Income Inequality in East Europe", *Artha-Vijnana*, Sept. 1986.

5. Kakwani, N.C., *Income Inequality and Poverty*, Oxford University Press, New Delhi, 1980, p. 63.

6. Kravis (1962), p. 99.

3

Saving and Investment

In this chapter, we shall examine the saving and investment behaviour of the sample households during the reference period. Having discussed the various aspects of the asset structure of these households it would be only natural that we go into the various aspects of the process whereby the assets have come to be accumulated. An analytical limitation of a cross section study in this respect obviously comes to light at this juncture, namely, that the assets available during the reference period have been due to the investment during the preceding period. Saving and investment of the households during the reference period can only explain the current variations in the stock of assets. However, in the sense in which and to the extent to which we are concerned in this study with this aspect, an analysis of the reference period's saving-investment behaviour would be deemed adequate.

Households investment has been defined[1] as the net addition to stock of asset holding accumulated during the reference period. This is the same thing as saving (or net worth) during the reference period if capital transferred and net change in lending are not taken as a part of investment. In other words, investment is equal to saving plus inflow minus outflow of assets due to capital transfers and net change in liabilities.

Symbolically,

$$S = I - T - \Delta L \qquad \text{...(4.1)}$$

where $S = \Delta A_p + \Delta A_f - \Delta L - T$

and $I = \Delta A_p + \Delta A_f$ ...(4.2)

where ΔL = net change in liabilities, T = net inflow of capital transfers, (inflow-outflow). ΔA_p and ΔA_f represent respectively the net change in physical and financial assets. Net Capital gains or losses due to appreciation or depreciation in the value of assets have been ignored.

An earlier specified, physical assets of the cultivator households comprise : land and its improvements, agricultural implements and machinery, farm and cattle-sheds, live-ctock, residential and non-residential buildings, business assets and consumer durables. Financial assets comprises : bank deposits, shares and securities, small savings including post office savings, premium paid to life insurance corporation and other such institutions, gold and jewellery, and miscellaneous financial assets.

When an asset is purchased or constructed, payment made either in cash or in kind is taken into consideration. When own material and family labour are used in construction these are suitably valued and added to investment. No adjustment is, however, made for capital damages in deriving gross investment. Thus gross investment is measured as difference between (a) acquisition of and additions to assets (physical as well as financial) owned by the cultivator households through purchases constructions, improvement and receipts from others, and (b) liquidation and transfer of assets to other cultivator households. Net investment in assets is arrived at by deducting the estimated amount of depreciation. Thus, for the purposes of obtaining saving and investment estimates in the present study, flows rather than stocks (both at the beginning and at the end of the period) have been considered in view of the data limitations (cross-section data).

We shall now attempt to find out the extent and pattern of investment with respect to the differences in the size, income, wealth and level of education within each category.

Gross Investment

The volume and composition of gross investment have been found to vary significantly across the difference categories of rural households. Table 3.1 reveals that large farmers contribute 51.33 per cent to total gross investment, small farmers 28.61 per cent, and medium farmers the remaining 20.06 per cent, i.e. minimum among the three categories. The share of physical investment to total investment in the case of large farmers is higher (28.57 per cent) in comparison to the medium and small farmers. The share of physical investment in the case of medium farmers is the lowest, i.e., 10.79 per cent. The share of financial investment in the total investment is also the highest 22.76 per cent, in the case of large farmers compared to the medium (9.27 per cent) and the small farmers (7.85 per cent).

Table 3.1
Total Gross Investment of Cultivator Households by Components
(In Percentage)

Type of Farmers	Physical Investment	Financial Investment	Total Investment
Large Farmers	28.57	22.76	51.33
Medium Farmers	10.79	9.27	20.06
Small Farmers	20.76	7.85	28.61
All Farmers	60.12	39.88	100.00

The foregoing behaviour of physical and financial investment reveals that investment both in the physical and in the financial assets is the highest in the case of large farmers which is mainly atributable to their scale of farming as well as to their income level. These households put a substantial part of their income in both types of investments.The lowest percentage of physical investment in the case of medium farmers may be due to their attraction for financial assets as they find an easy resort in this type of investment.

Net Investment

Table 3.2 brings out the composition of net investment of the sample households. The proportion of net investment to total net investment is the highest, 52.46 per cent, in the case of large cultivator house-holds and the lowest, 19.40 per cent, in the case of the medium. The proportion of net physical investment to total net investment is 21.65 per cent in the case of the large farmers 17.51 per cent among the small farmers and 6.84 per cent, the lowest, among the medium farmers. The share of net financial investment is much higher in the case of large, being 30.82 per cent, and quite low in the case of medium (12.56 per cent) and small farmers (10.62 per cent). For all households taken together, the net financial investment constitutes 54 per cent as against the physical investment which constitute the remaining 46 per cent of the total net investment.

Table 3.2
Total Net Investment of Cultivator Households by Components
(In Percentage)

Type of Farmers	Net Physical Investment	Net Financial Investment	Total Net Investment
Large Farmers	21.65	30.82	52.46
Medium Farmers	6.84	12.56	19.40
Small Farmers	17.51	10.62	28.14
All Farmers	46.00	54.00	100.00

Table 3.3 shows that livestock, agricultural implements and machinery, and buildings are the three major items into which the investible surplus is channelized by the cultivator households in Haryana. Investment in agricultural implements and machinery attract 24.79 per cent of total physical investment, which is clearly an indication of the extent to which modernisation and mechanisation of agricultural operations has been carried out in Haryana. Buildings also account for a significant proportion, 24.48 per cent, of the total physical investment. However, the investment in livestock attracts as much as 26.22 per cent of the total physical investment which indicates the continued importance of this asset in the production process in the State's agriculture. The shares of land, consumer durables, farm houses and cattle-sheds, and business assets are next in order.

Table 3.3 also shows the investment pattern of the three categories of cultivator households and their respective shares in the total physical investment. In the case of large farmers, the percentage shares of agricltural implements and machinery, buildings, and land are larger than those of the other components of physical investment. In the case of medium farmers the percentage shares of live-stock is higher (5.04 per cent) followed by agricultural implements and machinery 4.65 and land 4.56. In the case of small farmers the percentage shares of livestock and buildings are relatively higher, than the other components of physical investment, being 13.38 and 11.91 respectively. Agricultural implements and machinery comes next being 7.18 per cent.

Table 3.4 shows the composition of net financial investment of different categories of cultivator households. On the whole, percentage shares of bank deposits and of gold and jewellery in total net financial investment are higher, i.e. 78.58 per cent and 11.81 per cent respectively, than those of the other components of net financial investment. The percentage share of net financial investment

Table 3.3
Composition of Net Physical Investment of Cultivator Households
(In Rs.)

Components of Physical Investment	Large Farmers	Medium Farmers	Small Farmers	All Farmers
1. Land	476000 (10.34)	210000 (4.56)	17000 (0.37)	703000 (15.27)
2. Agriculture Implements and Machinery	596950 (12.96)	214250 (4.65)	330325 (7.18)	114152 (24.79)
3. Farm Houses and Cattle Sheds	91100 (1.98)	35500 (0.77)	113000 (0.28)	139600 (3.03)
4. Buildings	485000 (10.53)	93500 (2.03)	548500 (11.91)	1127000 (24.48)
5. Business Assets	59000 (1.28)	— (–)	— (–)	59000 (1.28)
6. Live Stock	359400 (7.80)	232000 (5.04)	616000 (13.38)	1207400 (26.22)
7. Consumer Durables	120475 (2.62)	41250 (0.90)	65450 (1.42)	227175 (4.93)
Total	2187925 (47.51)	826500 (17.95)	1590275 (34.54)	4604700 (100.00)

Note: Figures in parentheses denote the percentage share to total net physical investments of cultivator households.

Table 3.4
Composition of Net Financial Investment of Cultivator Households
(In Rs.)

Components of Investment	Large Farmers	Medium Farmers	Small Farmers	All Farmers
1. Bank deposits	1355200	58680	458000	2400000
	(44.37)	(19.21)	(14.99)	(78.58)
2. Shares and Securities	106000	34000	35000	175000
	(3.47)	(1.12)	(1.15)	(5.72)
3. Small Savings	64000	-	-	64000
	(2.09)	(-)	(-)	(2.10)
4. Premium Paid LIC.	21640	8020	24950	54610
	(0.71)	(0.26)	(0.81)	(1.79)
5. Gold and Jewellery	196300	81500	83000	360800
	(6.43)	(2.67)	(2.72)	(11.81)
Total	1743140	710320	600950	3054410
	(57.07)	(23.26)	(19.67)	(100)

Note: Figures in parentheses denote the percentage share to total net investment.

in the form of premium paid to the LIC is relatively low in all the three categories of cultivator households.

It is interesting to note that the net financial investment in small savings have been made only by large farmers and the other two categories, i.e., medium and small farmers, have not made any investment on this component. The behaviour of net financial investment shows that it is the large farmers whose share in almost all the items are higher than those of the other two categories.

Investment Distribution by Income Level

Table 3.5 and 3.6 reveal the distribution of net physical investment and net financial investment by income level in different categories of cultivator households.

Table 3.5
Net Physical Investment by Income Level (In Rs.)

Income Level	Large Farmers		Medium Farmers		Small Farmers		All Farmers	
	Number	Amount	Number	Amount	Number	Amount	Number	Amount
0 - 10000	-	-	-	-	5 (2.73)	11062 (1.11)	5 (1.56)	11062 (0.43)
10001 - 20000	-	-	-	-	49 (26.77)	251775 (25.42)	49 (15.31)	251775 (9.69)
20001 - 30000	1 (1.41)	7240 (0.59)	10 (15.15)	79217 (20.47)	61 (33.33)	334060 (33.73)	72 (22.50)	420517 (16.16)
Sub total	1 (1.41)	7240 (0.59)	10 (15.15)	79217 (20.47)	115 (62.83)	983856 (60.26)	126 (39.37)	683354 (26.27)
30001 - 40000	8 (11.27)	151402 (12.37)	19 (28.79)	54736 (14.15)	34 (18.58)	143515 (14.49)	61 (19.06)	349653 (13.44)
40001 - 50000	4 (5.63)	34420 (2.81)	18 (27.27)	106815 (27.60)	17 (9.29)	132725 (13.40)	39 (12.19)	273960 (10.53)
50001 - 60000	9 (12.68)	158001 (12.91)	7 (10.60)	75061 (19.40)	12 (6.56)	94053 (9.50)	28 (8.75)	327115 (12.57)
60001 - 70000	7 (9.86)	132543 (10.83)	5 (7.58)	53300 (13.77)	3 (1.64)	18896 (1.91)	15 (4.69)	204739 (7.67)
Sub total	28 (39.44)	476366 (38.92)	49 (74.24)	289912 (74.92)	66 (36.07)	389189 (39.30)	143 (44.69)	1155467 (44.41)
70001 - 80000	10 (14.08)	134400 (10.98)	1 (1.52)	12940 (3.34)	1 (0.55)	4030 (0.41)	12 (3.75)	151370 (5.82)
80001 - 90000	12 (16.90)	216393 (17.68)	2 (3.03)	17210 (4.45)	1 (0.55)	390 (0.03)	15 (4.69)	233993 (8.99)
90001 & Above	20 (28.17)	389668 (31.83)	4 (6.06)	-12320 (-3.18)	-	-	24 (5.50)	377348 (14.51)
Sub Total	42 (59.15)	740461 (60.49)	7 (10.61)	17830 (4.61)	2 (1.10)	4420 (0.44)	51 (15.94)	762711 (29.32)
All Income Levels	71 (100.00)	1224067 (100.00)	66 (100.00)	386959 (100.00)	183 (100.00)	990506 (100.00)	320 (100.00)	2601532 (100.00)

Note: Figures in Parentheses indicate percentage.

Table 3.6
Net Financial Investment of Cultivator Households by Income Level
(In Rs.)

Income Level	Large Farmers Number	Large Farmers Amount	Medium Farmers Number	Medium Farmers Amount	Small Farmers Number	Small Farmers Amount	All Farmers Number	All Farmers Amount
0 - 10000	-	-	-	-	5 (2.73)	13200 (2.20)	5 (1.56)	13200 (0.43)
10001 - 20000	-	-	-	-	49 (26.77)	14800 (19.10)	49 (15.31)	114800 (3.76)
20001 - 30000	1 (1.41)	9600 (0.55)	10 (15.15)	99000 (13.94)	61 (33.33)	172840 (28.76)	72 (22.50)	281440 (9.21)
Sub total	1 (1.41)	9600 (0.55)	10 (15.15)	99000 (13.94)	115 (62.83)	300840 (50.06)	126 (39.37)	409440 (13.40)
30001 - 40000	8 (11.27)	126000 (7.23)	19 (28.79)	144400 (20.33)	34 (18.58)	91970 (15.31)	61 (19.06)	362370 (11.86)
40001 - 50000	4 (5.63)	63500 (3.64)	18 (27.27)	141900 (19.98)	17 (9.29)	111200 (18.50)	39 (12.19)	316600 (10.37)
50001 - 60000	9 (12.68)	177600 (10.19)	7 (10.60)	88100 (12.40)	12 (6.56)	59440 (9.00)	28 (8.75)	325140 (10.65)
60001 - 70000	7 (9.86)	117500 (6.74)	5 (7.58)	67720 (9.53)	3 (1.64)	25300 (4.21)	15 (4.69)	210520 (6.89)
Sub total	28 (39.44)	484600 (27.80)	49 (74.24)	442120 (62.24)	66 (36.07)	287910 (47.91)	143 (44.69)	1214630 (39.77)
70001 - 80000	10 (14.08)	197300 (11.32)	1 (1.52)	7000 (0.99)	1 (0.55)	5000 (0.83)	12 (3.75)	209300 (6.85)
80001 - 90000	12 (19.60)	258400 (14.82)	2 (3.03)	12000 (1.69)	1 (0.55)	7200 (1.20)	15 (4.69)	277600 (9.09)
90001 & Above	20 (28.17)	7932240 (45.51)	4 (6.06)	150200 (21.14)	-	-	24 (7.50)	943440 (30.89)
Sub Total	42 (59.15)	1248940 (71.65)	7 (10.61)	169200 (23.82)	2 (1.10)	12200 (2.03)	51 (15.94)	1430340 (46.83)
All Income Level	71 (100.00)	1743140 (100.00)	66 (100.00)	710320 (100.00)	183 (100.00)	600950 (100.00)	320 (100.00)	3054410 (100.00)

Note: Figures in parentheses denote percentages.

The cultivator households have been divided into three income groups, viz., Rs. 0-30000, Rs. 30001-70000, and Rs. 70001 and above. In the case of large farmers, as the income level increases, both the physical and the financial investment increases. This is rather expectedly so. However, in the case of medium farmers, we find that both the physical and financial investments increase with increase in income level upto a point, but these tend decreases as the level of income goes beyond it. Interestingly, in the case of large farmers and medium farmers, the percentage share of net physical investment is relatively higher and that of the net financial investment lower upto middle income group (Rs. 30001-70000). The behaviour of small cultivator households is rather perplexing. In their case, both the physical and the financial investments decrease as we move up along the income ladder.

Thus, we find that the behaviour of investment vis-a-vis income level is consistent and positive in the case of large cultivator households. It is consistent but negataive in the case of small farm households. And it is erratic in the case of medium farmhouseholds.

Examined in aggregate terms, we find that the total net physical investment increases as we move from the lower income group to the middle income, but it tends to decrease as we move from the middle income group to higher income group. On the othe hand, the net financial investment increases continuously as we move up from one income group to the other. For total investment (net physical investment + net financial investment) taken as a whole, we find that it increases as we move from lower to the middle income group, but decreases as we move from the middle to the higher income group (Table 3.7).

Investment Distribution by Asset Level

Tables 3.8 and 3.9 reveal the distribution of net physical investment and net financial investment by

Table 3.7

Total Net Investment Distribution of Cultivator Households by Income Level

Income Level	Large Farmers Number	Large Farmers Amount	Medium Farmers Number	Medium Farmers Amount	Small Farmers Number	Small Farmers Amount	All Farmers Number	All Farmers Amount
0 - 10000	-	-	-	-	5 (2.73)	24262 (1.52)	5 (1.56)	24262 (0.43)
10001 - 20000	-	-	-	-	49 (26.77)	366575 (23.03)	49 (15.31)	366575 (6.48)
20001 - 30000	1 (1.41)	16840 (0.57)	10 (15.15)	178217 (16.24)	61 (33.33)	506900 (31.85)	72 (22.50)	701957 (12.41)
Sub total	1 (1.41)	16840 (0.57)	10 (15.15)	178217 (16.24)	115 (62.83)	897737 (56.40)	126 (39.37)	109274 (19.32)
30001 - 40000	8 (11.27)	277402 (9.35)	19 (28.79)	199136 (18.14)	34 (18.58)	235485 (14.80)	61 (19.06)	712023 (12.59)
40001 - 50000	4 (5.63)	97920 (3.30)	18 (27.27)	248715 (22.66)	17 (9.29)	243925 (15.33)	39 (12.19)	590560 (10.44)
50001 - 60000	9 (12.68)	335601 (11.31)	7 (10.60)	163161 (14.87)	12 (6.56)	153493 (9.64)	28 (8.75)	652255 (11.53)
60001 - 70000	7 (9.86)	250043 (8.43)	5 (7.58)	121020 (11.03)	3 (1.64)	44196 (2.79)	15 (4.69)	415259 (7.34)
Sub Total	28 (39.44)	960966 (32.39)	49 (74.24)	732032 (66.70)	66 (36.07)	677099 (42.55)	143 (44.69)	2370097 (41.90)
70001 - 80000	10 (14.08)	331700 (11.18)	1 (1.52)	19940 (1.82)	1 (0.55)	9030 (0.57)	12 (3.75)	360670 (6.38)
80001 - 90000	12 (16.90)	474793 (16.00)	2 (3.03)	29210 (2.67)	1 (0.55)	7590 (0.48)	15 (4.69)	511593 (9.05)
90001 - Above	20 (28.17)	1182908 (39.86)	4 (6.06)	137880 (12.57)	-	-	24 (7.50)	1320788 (23.35)
Sub total	42 (59.15)	1989401 (67.04)	7 (10.61)	187030 (17.06)	2 (1.10)	16620 (1.05)	51 (15.94)	2193051 (38.78)
All Income Levels	71 (100.00)	2967207 (100.00)	66 (100.00)	1097279 (100.00)	183 (100.00)	1591456 (100.00)	320 (100.00)	5655942 (100.00)

Note : Figures in Parentheses indicate percentages.

Table 3.8
Net Physical Investment of Cultivator Households by Asset Level
(In Rs.)

Income Level	Large Farmers		Medium Farmers		Small Farmers		All Farmers	
	Number of Households	Amount	Number of Households	Amount	Number of Households	Amount	Number of Households	Amount
Upto - 100000	-	-	-	-	11	57492	11	57492
					(6.01)	(5.80)	(3.44)	(2.21)
100001 - 200000	-	-	-	-	50	159922	50	159922
					(27.32)	(16.15)	(15.63)	(6.15)
200001 - 300000	1	650	-	-	75	436914	76	437564
	(1.41)	(0.05)			(40.99)	(44.11)	(23.75)	(16.82)
300001 - 400000	-	-	6	2886	30	230042	36	232928
			(9.09)	(0.75)	(16.40)	(23.23)	(11.25)	(8.95)
400001 - 500000	1	19132	18	96508	5	10496	24	126136
	(1.41)	(1.56)	(27.27)	(24.94)	(2.73)	(1.06)	(7.50)	(4.85)
Sub Total	2	19782	24	99394	171	894866	197	1014042
	(2.82)	(1.61)	(36.36)	(25.69)	(93.45)	(90.35)	(61.57)	(38.98)
500001 - 600000	-	-	19	96005	3	69029	22	165034
			(28.79)	(24.81)	(2.64)	(6.97)	(6.97)	(6.34)
600001 - 700000	4	25936	8	85460	2	10721	14	122117
	(5.63)	(2.12)	(12.12)	(22.09)	(1.09)	(1.08)	(4.37)	(4.69)
700001 - 800000	13	279827	5	90660	3	3900	21	374387
	(18.31)	(22.86)	(7.57)	(23.43)	(1.64)	(0.39)	(6.56)	(14.39)

(Continued...)

Income Level	Large Farmers		Medium Farmers		Small Farmers		All Farmers	
	Number of Households	Amount	Number of Households	Amount	Number of Households	Amount	Number of Households	Amount
800001 - 900000	9	73550	-	-	2	6820	11	80370
	(12.88)	(6.01)			(1.09)	0.69)	(3.44)	(3.09)
900001 - 1000000	8	129145	-	-	-	-	8	129145
	(11.27)	(10.55)					(2.50)	(4.97)
Sub Total	34	508458	32	272125	10	90470	76	871053
	(47.89)	(41.54)	(48.48)	(70.33)	(5.46)	(9.13)	(23.74)	(33.48)
1000001 - 1500000	15	257885	8	-2240	2	5170	25	260815
	(21.13)	(21.07)	(12.12)	(-0.58)	(1.09)	(0.52)	(7.81)	(10.03)
1500001 - 2000000	10	92238	1	12940	-	-	11	105178
	(14.08)	(7.54)	(1.52)	(3.34)			(3.44)	(4.04)
2000001 & Above	10	345704	1	4740	-	-	11	350444
	(14.08)	(56.85)	(1.52)	(1.22)			(3.44)	(13.47)
Sub Total	35	695827	10	15440	2	5170	47	716437
	(45.29)	(56.85)	(15.16)	(3.98)	(1.09)	(0.52)	(14.69)	(27.54)
All Asset Levels	71	1224067	66	386959	183	990506	320	2601532
	(100.00)	(100.00)	(100.00)	(100.00)	(100.00)	(100.00)	(100.00)	(100.00)

Note: Figures in parentheses indicate percentages.

Table 3.9
Net Financial Investment of Cultivator Households by Asset Level
(In Rs.)

Income Level	Large Farmers		Medium Farmers		Small Farmers		All Farmers	
	Number of Households	Amount	Number of Households	Amount	Number of Households	Amount	Number of Households	Amount
Upto - 100000	-	-	-	-	11	23240	11	23240
					(6.01)	(3.37)	(3.44)	(0.76)
100001 - 200000	-	-	-	-	50	163310	50	163310
					(27.32)	(27.18)	(15.63)	(5.35)
200001 - 300000	1	32000	-	-	75	186500	76	218500
	(1.41)	(1.84)			(40.99)	(31.03)	(23.75)	(7.15)
300001 - 400000	-	-	6	64000	30	136800	36	200800
			(9.09)	(9.01)	(16.40)	(22.76)	(11.25)	(6.57)
400001 - 500000	1	10000	18	117200	5	40300	24	167500
	(1.41)	(0.57)	(27.27)	(16.50)	(2.73)	(6.71)	(7.50)	(5.48)
Sub Total	2	42000	24	181200	171	550150	197	773350
	(2.82)	(2.41)	(36.36)	(25.51)	(93.45)	(91.55)	(61.57)	(25.31)
500001 - 600000	-	-	19	154200	3	3500	22	157700
			(28.79)	(21.71)	(1.64)	(0.58)	(6.87)	(5.16)
600001 - 700000	4	53600	8	176200	32	10800	14	240600
	(5.63)	(3.07)	(12.12)	(24.81)	(1.09)	(1.80)	(4.37)	(7.88)
700001 - 800000	13	129600	5	85000	3	10800	21	225400
	(18.31)	(7.44)	(7.57)	(11.96)	(1.64)	(1.80)	(6.56)	(7.38)

(Continued....)

Income Level	Large Farmers Number of Households	Large Farmers Amount	Medium Farmers Number of Households	Medium Farmers Amount	Small Farmers Number of Households	Small Farmers Amount	All Farmers Number of Households	All Farmers Amount
800001 - 900000	9	133700	-	-	2	14500	11	148200
	(12.68)	(7.67)			(1.09)	(2.41)	(3.44)	(4.85)
900001 - 1000000	8	155000	-	-	-	-	8	155000
	(11.27)	(8.89)					(2.50)	(5.08)
Sub Total	34	471900	32	415400	10	39600	76	926900
	(47.89)	(27.07)	(48.48)	(58.48)	(5.46)	(6.59)	(23.74)	(30.35)
1000001 - 1500000	15	359000	8	91000	2	11200	25	461200
	(21.13)	(20.60)	(2.12)	(12.81)	(1.09)	(1.86)	(7.81)	(15.10)
1500001 - 2000000	10	292340	1	7000	-	-	11	299340
	(14.08)	(16.77)	(1.52)	(0.99)			(3.44)	(09.80)
2000001 & Above	10	577900	1	15720	-	-	11	593620
	(14.08)	(33.15)	(1.52)	(2.21)			(3.44)	(19.44)
Sub Total	35	1229240	10	113720	2	11200	47	1354160
	(45.29)	(70.52)	(15.10)	(16.01)	(1.09)	(1.86)	(14.69)	(44.34)
All Asset Levels	71	1743140	66	710320	183	600950	320	3054410
	(100.00)	(100.00)	(100.00)	(100.00)	(100.00)	(100.00)	(100.00)	(100.00)

Note: Figures in parentheses indicate percentages.

asset level. Assets have been classified into ranges : (i) upto Rs.500000, (ii) from Rs. 500001 to Rs.1000000 and (iii) Rs. 1000001 and above.

In the case of large farmers, investment (physical as well as financial) increases as we move from the lower income level to the higher, revealing a positive and consistent relationship between asset level and investment. In the case of medium farmers, investment (physical as well as financial) increases as we move from the low asset-level to the middle asset level, but it declines as we move from the middle asset level to higher asset level, revealing an erratic relationship. In the case of small farmers, we find that the investment decreases as we move from the lower asset level to the higher. The interesting inference is that the investment behaviour is negatively influenced by the asset level of the cultivator households. The more they have of these assets, the less they want to have more of these.

On the whole, net physical investement decreases as we move from the lower asset group to higher. For all cultivator households taken together, we found an increasing trend in financial investment as we move from the first asset level to the second and then to the third asset level. In aggregate terms, total net investment (net physical investment + netfinancial investment) as revealed in Table 3.10, follows the same pattern as in the case of both the net physical investment and the net financial investment in different categories of cultivator households. Thus, both in relation to the income levels and in relation to the asset levels, the investment behaviour of the different size groups of the farm households is quite parallel.

Investment Distribution by Education Level

We now examine the role of education in shaping the investment behaviour of a household. Table 3.11 and

Table 3.10
Total Net Investment Distribution of Cultivator Households by Asset-Level
(In Rs.)

Income Level	Large Farmers		Medium Farmers		Small Farmers		All Farmers	
	Number of Households	Amount	Number of Households	Amount	Number of Households	Amount	Number of Households	Amount
Upto - 100000	-	-	-	-	11	80732	11	80732
					(6.01)	(5.07)	(3.44)	(1.43)
100001 - 200000	-	-	-	-	50	323232	50	323232
					(27.32)	(20.31)	(15.63)	(5.71)
200001 - 300000	1	32650	-	-	75	623414	76	656064
	(1.41)	(1.10)			(40.99)	(39.17)	(23.75)	(11.60)
300001 - 400000	-	-	6	66886	30	366842	36	433728
			(9.09)	(6.10)	(16.40)	(23.05)	(11.25)	(7.67)
400001 - 500000	1	29132	18	213708	5	50796	24	293636
	(1.41)	(0.98)	(27.27)	(19.48)	(2.73)	(3.20)	(7.50)	(5.19)
Sub Total	2	61782	24	280594	171	1445016	197	1787392
	(2.82)	(2.08)	(36.36)	(25.58)	(93.45)	(90.80)	(61.57)	(31.60)
500001 - 600000	-	-	19	250205	3	72529	22	322734
			(28.79)	(22.80)	(1.64)	(4.56)	(6.87)	(5.71)
600001 - 700000	4	79536	8	261660	2	21521	14	362717
	(5.63)	(2.68)	(12.12)	(23.85)	(1.09)	(1.35)	(4.37)	(6.41)
700001 - 800000	13	409427	5	175660	3	14700	21	599787
	(18.31)	(13.80)	(7.57)	(16.00)	(1.64)	(0.92)	(6.56)	(10.61)

(Continued...)

Income Level	Large Farmers		Medium Farmers		Small Farmers		All Farmers	
	Number of Households	Amount	Numbe of Households	Amount	Number of Households	Amount	Number of Households	Amount
800001 - 900000	9	207250	-	-	2	21320	11	228570
	(12.68)	(6.98)			(1.09)	(1.34)	(3.44)	(4.04)
900001 - 1000000	8	284145	-	-	-	-	8	284145
	(11.27)	(9.58)					(2.50)	(5.02)
Sub Total	34	980358	32	687525	10	130070	76	1797953
	(47.89)	(33.04)	(48.48)	(62.65)	(5.46)	(8.17)	(23.74)	(31.79)
1000001 - 1500000	15	616885	8	88760	2	16370	25	722015
	(21.13)	(20.79)	(12.12)	(8.09)	(1.09)	(1.03)	(7.81)	(12.77)
1500000 - 2000000	10	384578	1	19940	-	-	11	404518
	(14.08)	(12.96)	(1.52)	(1.82)			(3.44)	(7.15)
2000000 & Above	10	923604	1	20460	-	-	11	944064
	(14.08)	(31.13)	(1.52)	(1.86)			(3.44)	(16.69)
Sub Total	35	1925067	10	129160	2	16370	47	2070547
	(45.29)	(64.88)	(15.16)	(11.77)	(1.09)	(1.03)	(14.69)	(36.61)
All Asset Levels	71	2967207	66	1097279	183	1591456	320	5655942
	(100.00)	(100.00)	(100.00)	(100.00)	(100.00)	(100.00)	(100.00)	(100.00)

Note: Figures in parentheses indicate the percentages.

3.12 reveal the distribution of net physical investment and net financial investment by education levels of the chief earner of the cultivator household. Of the total physical investment, households with chief earner who had no formal education account for 55.82 per cent, those who had education upto primary level account for 11.46 per cent and those who had education upto middle standard account for 10.46 per cent. However, household with chief earner who had education upto matriculation level account for 18.40 per cent of the total net physical investment. Chief earner having education upto gradulate level of above account for just 3.86 per cent. There is similar pattern of net physical investment in case of large and small farmers.

Table 3.12 shows that net financial investment for all households taken together follows the same pattern as of net physical investment in the case of the medium farmers. But in the case of large farmers, there is a variation in the pattern in that the percentage share of investment in total net financial investment is not the lowest in the higher education level. From the above analysis it reveals that households with chief earner who had higher education (graduate and above) invest more in financial assets than in physical assets.

Table 3.13 shows the distribution of total net investment (net physical investment plus net financial investment) by education level. In aggregate term, i.e., all farmers taken together, the investment trend is different (from the net physical and net financial investment trends) and follows the pattern of net financial investment experienced by the small farmers. Category-wise, the large farmers and the small farmers show the same trend as is in the case of financial investment relating to these two category, but the trend experienced by the medium farmers does not resemble with that of the trends experienced by it in the case of net financial or net physical investment. This signifies that level of education does not play any consistently crucial role in this respect.

Table 3.11
Net Physical Investment by Education Level

Education Level	Large Farmers		Medium Farmers		Small Farmers		All Farmers	
	Number of Households	Amount	Number of Households	Amount	Number of Households	Amount	Number of Households	Amount
1. No formal Education	40	606219	42	190504	119	655387	201	1452110
	(56.34)	(49.53)	(63.64)	(49.23)	(65.03)	(66.17)	(62.81)	(55.82)
2. Complete Primary Education	10	158652	8	51660	15	87896	33	298208
	(14.08)	(12.96)	(12.12)	(13.35)	(8.20)	(8.87)	(10.31)	(11.46)
3. Complete Middle Education	9	120788	7	75005	16	76422	32	272215
	(12.68)	(9.87)	(10.61)	(19.38)	(8.74)	(7.72)	(10.00)	(10.46)
4. Complete Matric Education	7	258553	8	58300	29	161701	44	478554
	(9.86)	(21.12)	(12.12)	(15.07)	(15.85)	(16.32)	(13.75)	(18.40)
5. Graduate/Post Graduate Education	5	79855	1	11490	4	9100	10	100445
	(7.04)	(6.52)	(1.51)	(2.97)	(2.18)	(0.92)	(3.13)	(3.86)
All Education Level	71	1224067	66	386959	183	990506	320	2601532
	(100.00)	(100.00)	(100.00)	(100.00)	(100.00)	(100.00)	(100.00)	(100.00)

Note: Figures in parentheses indicate percentages.

Table 3.12
Net Financial Investment by Education Level

Education Level	Large Farmers		Medium Farmers		Small Farmers		All Farmers	
	Number of Households	Amount	Number of Households	Amount	Number of Households	Amount	Number of Households	Amount
1. No formal Education	40 (56.34)	880240 (50.50)	42 (63.64)	395500 (55.68)	119 (65.03)	397870 (66.21)	201 (62.81)	1673610 (54.79)
2. Complete Primary Education	10 (14.08)	254550 (14.60)	8 (12.12)	69200 (9.74)	15 (8.20)	35200 (5.86)	23 (10.31)	358950 (11.75)
3. Complete Middle Education	9 (12.68)	170950 (9.81)	7 (10.61)	172500 (24.29)	16 (8.74)	79600 (13.24)	32 (10.00)	423050 (13.85)
4. Complete Matric Education	7 (9.86)	219500 (12.59)	8 (12.12)	68420 (9.63)	29 (15.85)	79780 (13.28)	44 (13.75)	367700 (12.04)
5. Graduate/Post-Graduate Education	5 (7.04)	217900 (12.50)	1 (1.51)	4700 (0.66)	4 (2.10)	8500 (1.41)	10 (3.13)	231100 (7.57)
All Education Level	71 (100.00)	1743140 (100.00)	66 (100.00)	710320 (100.00)	183 (100.00)	600950 (100.00)	320 (100.00)	3054410 (100.00)

Note : Figures in perentheses denote percentages.

Table 3.13
Total Net Investment Distribution by Education Level

Education Level	Large Farmers		Medium Farmers		Small Farmers		All Farmers	
	Number of Households	Amount	Number of Households	Amount	Number of Households	Amount	Number of Households	Amount
1. No formal Education	40 (56.34)	1486459 (50.10)	42 (63.64)	586004 (53.41)	119 (65.03)	1053257 (66.18)	201 (62.81)	3125720 (55.27)
2. Complete Primary Education	10 (14.08)	413202 (13.93)	8 (12.12)	120860 (7.73)	15 (8.20)	123096 (7.73)	33 (10.31)	657158 (11.62)
3. Complete Middle Education	9 (12.68)	291738 (9.83)	7 (10.61)	247505 (22.56)	16 (8.74)	156022 (9.81)	32 (10.00)	695265 (12.29)
4. Complete Matric Education	7 (9.86)	478053 (16.11)	8 (12.12)	126720 (11.55)	29 (15.85)	241481 (15.17)	44 (13.75)	846254 (14.96)
5. Graduate / Post-Graduate Education	5 (7.04)	297755 (10.03)	1 (1.51)	16190 (1.47)	4 (2.18)	17600 (1.11)	10 (3.13)	331545 (5.86)
All Education Level	71 (100.00)	2967207 (100.00)	66 (100.00)	1097279 (100.00)	183 (100.00)	1591456 (100.00)	320 (100.00)	5655942 (100.00)

Note: Figures in parentheses denote percentages.

Determinants of Investment by Cultivator Households

In the present study, the income level, asset level, number of earners in the family, age of the chief earner, size of family, level of education of the chief earner (average year of schooling) have been selected for analysis as the socio-economic determinants of the investment by the cultivator households. Since the analysis in terms of the linear function did not yield significant results, the following semi-log functional form was used for more meaningful results:

$$I = f(x_1, x_2, x_3, x_4, x_5, x_6) \qquad ...(3.3)$$

where I = Investment

x_1 = Income Level

x_2 = Asset Level

x_3 = Age of the chief earner

x_4 = Number of earners

x_5 = Size of family

x_6 = Education Level (Average year of Schooling)

We specify education (3.3) above as the following semi-log function.

$$I = a + b_1 \log x_1 + b_2 \log x_2 + b_3 \log x_3 + b_4 \log x_4 + b_5 \log x_5 + b_6 \log x_6$$

Table 3.14 reveals the relationship of investment with the selected socio-economic factors, viz., income, asset, age of chief earner, number of earners, size of family and education. Four regression equations with semi-log have been estimated for each of the three categories of cultivator households and one for the total cultivator households. The estimated co-efficients, their associated 't' values and R^2 have been presented in Table.

Table 3.14
Estimated Investment Relations

Type of Farmers	Constant (b_o)	x_1	x_2	x_3	x_4	x_5	x_6	R^2
Large Farmers	2.7312	.0679* (2.68935)	.1570 (1.29452)	-.0255 (-.83759)	.2693** (2.35396)	-.3594* (-3.58762)	.1181* (2.78652)	.54
Medium Farmers	1.9876	.1023* (4.83146)	.0936 (.76293)	.0035 (.98317)	.1013** (1.98353)	-.0984* (-2.79432)	.2164* (3.11773)	.38
Small Farmers	0.1024	.0192*** (1.89253)	-.02316 (-.69358)	-.1237** (-2.58353)	.0143** (1.98867)	-.1695* (-3.63985)	.0037 (.93245)	.69
All Farmers	1.9245	.1736* (4.40346)	.1096 (.23189)	-.0856** (-2.89682)	.1163 (.89693)	-.0389* (-6.73275)	.1332** (2.11591)	.74

Note: Figures in parentheses denote 't' values.
* Regression coefficient is significant at 1 per cent level of significance.
** Regression coefficient is significant at 5 per cent level of significance.
*** Regression coefficient is significant at 10 per cent level of significance.

An examination of the Table reveals that among the various factors which determine the level of investment, income has been one of the major determinants positively contributing to investment for all categories of cultivator households. Investment has been found to be negatively related to the age of chief earner (except in the case of medium farmers) and size of family for all categories. Investment has positive relationship with asset level except in the case of small farmers. Education of the chief earner has a positive relationship for all categories taken separately and as a whole. The number of earners has also been found to have a positive relation in this regard.

The explanatory variables considered here explain 38 per cent to 74 per cent of the variations in investment. The intercept has been found to be positive for all categories of cultivator households. This implies that investment is taking place even at the zero level of disposable income which is consistent with the accecpted theory. We know that a household makes investment from three sources, viz., current saving, past savings and borrowings. The households make investment in enlarging their activities by borrowing even though they have zero level of disposable income. It clearly brings out the healthy attitude of farmers in the State towards taking risk for capital formation.

Section II

The present section has been devoted to a detailed analysis of the volume of savings, its distribution, the role of socio-economic and demographic factors in the determination of savings and attitudes towards, and motivations for, savings. In so far as savings provide the wherewithal for invesment, it would be more logical to take up the discussion of savings before the discussion of the formation of assets during the year. However, the reverse sequence as adopted in this chapter is more proper in view of the adoption of the balance sheet approach for the estimation of savings in the present study. Gross savings (or the change in the net worth) are taken as the change in net assets (physical as well as financial) minus the net change in liabilities (i.e., borrowings minus debt repayments) and the transfer inflows during the period. Net savings have been estimated by deducting depreciation from the gross savings. The method of estimating depreciation and other issues related with the measurement of savings has been discussed in Chapter One. Table 3.15 presents estimates of both gross and net savings for different categories of cultivator households.

The large farmers contribute the bulk of the total savings, gross as well as net savings. They save as much as 54.74 per cent of the gross savings and 57.96 per cent of the net savings. As against this, the share of small farmers is 26.51 per cent and 24.84 per cent, respectively. Savings by medium farmers are lower in comparison, being 18.75 per cent (gross) and 17.20 per cent (net). The dominant position of the large farm households would seem to be due mainly to their disapproportionately large shares in total assets, physical as well as financial, as already seen in the preceding chapter.

Saving Distribution by Income Level

Table 3.16 depicts the saving distribution by income level among different categories of sample households. Income is divided into three groups. Rs. 0 - 30000, Rs. 30001 - 70000 and Rs. 70001 and above. In the case of large farmers, as income increases savings also increase. In the case of medium farmers, savings increase as we move from the low income group to the middle income group and fall when we move from the middle income group to the higher income group. Contrary to the received theory of consumption, we find that in the case of small farmers, saving falls consistently as income level increases. But, of course, this result would seem to due partly to the relative number of households in the various income brackets in the small size categories.

Table 3.15
Estimation of Gross and Net Saving for Different Categories of Cultivator Households

Items	Large Farmers	Medium Farmers	Small Farmers	All Farmers
1. Change in Physical Assets (ΔA_p)	2187925	826500	1590275	4604700
2. Change in Financial Assets (ΔA_f)	743140	710320	600950	3054410
3. Net Change in Liabilities (ΔL)	529000	410000	583500	1522500
4. Net in Flow of Capital Transfer (T) (In-flow-out-flow)	52900	-20760	-14200	18030
5. Gross Saving (1+2-3-4)	3349165 (54.74)	1147490 (18.75)	1621925 (26.51)	6118580 (100)
6. Depreciation	963858	439541	599769	2003168
7. Net Saving (5-6)	2385307 (57.96)	707949 (17.20)	1022156 (24.84)	4115412 (100)

Note: Figures in parentheses denote percentages.

Table 3.16
Net Saving Distribution by Income Level among Different categories of Cultivator Households (In Rs.)

Income Level	Large Farmers		Medium Farmers		Small Farmers		All Farmers	
	Number of Households	Amount	Number of Households	Amount	Number of Households	Amount	Number of Households	Amount
Upto - 10000	-	-	-	-	5	18262	5	18262
					(2.73)	(1.79)	(1.56)	(0.44)
10001 - 20000	-	-	-	-	49	225325	49	225325
					(26.77)	(22.04)	(15.31)	(5.48)
20001 - 30000	1	16840	10	114387	61	305750	72	436977
	(1.41)	(0.71)	(15.15)	(16.16)	(33.33)	(29.91)	(22.50)	(10.62)
Sub Total	1	16840	10	114387	115	549337	126	680564
	(1.41)	(0.71)	(15.15)	(16.16)	(62.83)	(53.74)	(39.37)	(16.54)
30001 - 40000	8	180902	19	122366	34	187585	61	470853
	(11.27)	(7.58)	(28.79)	(17.28)	(18.58)	(16.40)	(19.06)	(11.44)
40001 - 50000	4	119120	18	146165	17	184925	39	450210
	(5.63)	(4.99)	(27.27)	(20.65)	(9.29)	(18.09)	(12.19)	(10.94)
50001 - 60000	9	267101	7	92161	12	75493	28	434755
	(12.68)	(11.20)	(10.61)	(13.02)	(6.56)	(7.39)	(8.75)	(10.56)
60001 - 70000	7	230543	5	60840	3	28196	15	319579
	(9.86)	(9.66)	(7.58)	(8.59)	(1.64)	(2.76)	(4.69)	(7.77)
Sub Total	28	797666	49	421532	66	456199	143	1675397
	(39.44)	(33.43)	(74.24)	(59.54)	(36.07)	(44.64)	(44.69)	(40.71)

Income Level	Large Farmers		Medium Farmers		Small Farmers		All Farmers	
	Number of Households	Amount	Number of Households	Amount	Number of Households	Amount	Number of Households	Amount
70001 - 80000	10	284700	1	19940	1	9030	12	313670
	(14.08)	(11.94)	(1.51)	(2.82)	(0.55)	(0.88)	(3.75)	(7.62)
80001 - 90000	12	386793	2	14210	1	7590	15	408593
	(16.90)	(16.22)	(3.03)	(2.01)	(0.55)	(0.74)	(4.69)	(9.93)
90001 & Above	20	899308	4	137880	-	-	24	1037188
	(28.17)	(37.70)	(6.06)	(19.40)			(7.50)	(25.20)
Sub Total	42	1570801	07	172030	02	16620	51	1759451
	(59.15)	(65.86)	(10.61)	(29.30)	(1.10)	(1.62)	(15.94)	(42.75)
All Income Level	71	2385307	66	707949	183	1022156	320	4115412
	(100.00)	(100.00)	(100.00)	(100.00)	(100.00)	(100.00)	(100.00)	(100.00)

Note : Figures in parentheses denote percentages.

In the aggregate terms, however, the total svings increase as income increases, revealing a positive relationship between saving and income. In other words, because of their relative weight, the saving-income pattern of the large farmers more than neutralizes the inverse pattern of the small farmers and the rather erratic pattern of the medium farmers.

Saving Distribution by Level of Saving

Table 3.17 presents the distribution of cultivator households by level of saving and share in total savings. Interestingly and significantly, households command shares in the total savings quite disproportionate to their share in the household population - the bottom households save disporportionately less and the top households disproportionately more. The information given in Table 3.17 can be rearranged to see how the shares in population and in saving of the different house-hold groups at the bottom and the top behave. Among the cultivator households, on the one extreme are the vast majority of households (66.88 per cent) whose savings are rather meagre and constitute only 24.30 per cent of the total. Many of these households are dissavers, some do not save at all, and some save very little. And none of these save more than Rs. 10000 annually. Of the total households, 20 per cent house holds are those whose saving is not more than Rs. 25000 annually. On the other extreme stands a relatively small group of households, constituting 13.12 per cent of the total population, which commands a disproportionately high share in total savings, namely, 50.78 per cent. Each household of this group saves more than Rs. 25000 annually.

Size-wise, among the large farmers, the bottom 9.86 per cent households contribute only 1.88 per cent of the total savings. The middle (Rs. 10001-25000 annually) 36.62 per cent households in this size group contribute 19.37 per cent. The remaining top 53.52 per cent contribute an amazingly high proportion of 78.75 per cent

Table 3.17
Distribution of Cultivator Households by Levels of Net Saving and Type
(In Rs.)

Income Level	Large Farmers		Medium Farmers		Small Farmers		All Farmers	
	Number of Households	Amount	Number of Households	Amount	Number of Households	Amount	Number of Households	Amount
-5000 - 2500	-	-	2	-8635	1	-4110	3	-12745
	-	-	(3.03)	(-1.22)	(0.55)	(-0.40)	(0.94)	(-0.30)
-2500 - 1	-	-	2	-2790	9	-9217	11	-12007
			(3.03)	(-0.39)	(4.92)	(-0.90)	(3.44)	(-0.29)
1 - 1000	1	760	2	630	7	4859	10	6249
	(1.41)	(0.03)	(3.03)	(3.03)	(3.83)	(0.47)	(3.12)	(0.15)
1001 - 2000	-	-	1	1660	16	24487	17	26147
			(1.51)	(0.23)	(8.74)	(2.39)	(5.31)	(0.63)
2001 - 4000	-	-	3	8955	37	115264	40	124219
			(4.55)	(1.26)	(20.21)	(11.24)	(12.50)	(3.02)
4001 - 6000	2	9930	10	49852	51	255424	63	315206
	(2.82)	(0.42)	(15.15)	(7.04)	(27.87)	(24.92)	(19.69)	(7.65)
6001 - 10000	4	33982	25	199591	41	319430	70	553003
	(5.63)	(1.43)	(37.88)	(28.19)	(22.40)	(31.45)	(21.88)	(13.44)
Sub Total	7	44672	45	219263	162	706137	214	1000072
	(9.86)	(1.88)	(68.18)	(35.20)	(88.52)	(69.17)	(66.88)	(24.30)
10001 - 15000	9	113871	10	125921	13	146985	32	386777
	(12.68)	(4.77)	(15.15)	(17.79)	(7.10)	(14.34)	(10.00)	(9.40)

(Continued...)

Income Level	Large Farmers		Medium Farmers		Small Farmers		All Farmers	
	Number of Households	Amount	Numbe of Households	Amount	Number of Households	Amount	Number of Households	Amount
15001 - 20000	9	160990	5	88335	3	47660	17	296985
	(12.68)	(6.75)	(7.58)	(12.48)	(1.64)	(4.65)	(5.31)	(7.22)
20001 - 25000	8	187301	3	67535	4	87076	15	341912
	(11.26)	(7.85)	(4.55)	(9.54)	(2.19)	(8.49)	(4.69)	(8.30)
Sub Total	26	462162	18	281791	20	281721	64	1025674
	(36.62)	(19.37)	(27.28)	(39.81)	(10.93)	(27.48)	(20.00)	(24.92)
25001 - 50000	26	870675	2	63425	1	34298	29	968398
	(36.62)	(36.50)	(3.03)	(8.96)	(0.55)	(3.35)	(9.06)	(23.53)
50001 - & Above	12	1007798	1	113470	-	-	13	1121268
	(16.90)	(42.25)	(1.51)	(16.03)			(4.06)	(27.25)
Sub Total	38	1878473	3	176895	1	34298	42	2089666
	(53.52)	(78.75)	(4.54)	(24.99)	(0.55)	(3.35)	(13.12)	(50.78)
All Saving Levels	71	2385307	66	707949	183	1022156	320	4115412
	(100.00)	(100.00)	(100.00)	(100.00)	(100.00)	(100.00)	(100.00)	(100.00)

Note: Figures in parentheses indicate percentages.

to the total savings. In the medium size category, the bottom 68.18 per cent households have a 35.20 per cent share; the middle 27.28 per cent house-holds have a 39.81 per cent share; and the top 4.54 per cent households have a 24.99 per cent share in the total savings. Savings among the small farmers are more disporportionately distributed. Of the total households, the bottom 88.52 per cent have a 69.17 per cent share of total savings while the top 0.55 per cent contribute 3.53 per cent of the total svings.

This brings out the market disparities in the savings propensities of the different size and income categories of the farm households and in their relative shares in the total savings of the sector as a whole.

Determinants of Saving

We have seen that savings are more or less evenly distributed among cultivators in Haryana. We have also seen that income plays an important role in the determination of savings. The functional relationship between income and savings has, indeed, been both theoretically and empirically established. However, much disagreement among economists prevails on the relative importance of the other determinants of savings. Many economists are of the opinion that saving ratio is independent of the absolute level of income. According to them, the very first premise that saving is a function of income is an over simplification, especially, when the period involved is not too short.

Income is generally considered to be an important explanatory variable. There are different hypotheses based on different concepts of income, the more important being the 'absolute income hypothesis' of Keynes, the 'relative income hypothesis' of Duesenberry, and the 'permanent income hypothesis' of Friedman. Recent empirical research in the advanced countries like the U.S.A. and the U.K. had led some to conclude that income is not an influence "to which much weight should be given while attempting to explain saving behaviour[3]". The response of savings to a change in income is not symmetrical either,. as Friend (1954) concludes on the basis of the 1941-42 and post-war consumer survey in the USA. Lawrence Klein (1954) observes a significant influence, though retarding, on savings only with a decrease in income. Bhalla (1978) has conducted a study to test whether the source of income or the level of income is an important determinant of saving. Using Additional Rural Income (ARIS) data, he has found that it is the investment opportunity rather than the source of income which is important in determining the rate of saving.

Among the other factors affecting saving behaviour, the more important are lag of consumption behind income, building up of cash balances for transaction purposes, and the desire to set aside a portion of the current income for future use. The poor people have lower income as compared to those who are economically better off. The lower position of the poor households on the income scale induces them to raise their standard of living. This is due to the demonstration effect[4] created by the relatively higher income groups which income groups tends to raise the marginal propensity to consume of the poor and reduce their marginal propensity to save. When people come into contact with superior pattern of consumption or new ways of meeting old wants, they for a while have a feeling of restlessness and dissatisfaction. New desires are aroused, the propensity to consume is raised and the propensity to save is curtailed.

The importance of the impact of demographic variables on household saving behaviour has long been recognised. But not much empirical work has been undertaken in this direction, especially in developiong countries. Amongst the studies[5] that have been conducted in India, some have utilized household surveys as the data source where as others have used cross section data.

Among the demographic variables, the size of the household is an important factor accounting for variations in saving behaviour. Possibly the most widely investigated aspect of saving is the adverse impact of population on the availability of savings for capital formation. There are several connections to be examined between population growth and the supply of saving for investment. Attention is centered on the relationship between family size and rate of saving. The most commonly postulated association between family size and saving centres on the dependency rate 'adult equivalence' framework. For, given household income the consumption demands of children (of their adult equivalent consumption) yield a reduction in like amount in the level of household savings. This 'adult equivalent hypothesis' has been widely applied by Coale and Hoover (1958) for India. Kuznets (1960) finds that negative saving impact of large families is larger in less developed countries. In contrast, Gupta (1971) argues, that when income levels are very low, there is no margin left for saving. It simply means that people are sharing only poverty. Demographic factors, like dependency ratio, become operative only when the per capita income of the working population reaches a level where it can provide more than a minimum level of living, thus generating potential saving.

The other demographic factor relates to the age composition of a household. The larger the number of people in non-productive age groups, the greater the dependency ratio and the lower the saving performance. The underlying logic is that the too young and the too old members of the family do not add to income, while they do add to consumption with the result that saving is eroded. This aspect has been adequately incorporated by Ando and Modigliani (1954) in their 'life cycle hypothesis' of consumption. It is relevant to point out that both the high birth rate and the low death rate raise the dependency ratio[7].

Apart from these variables, level of education is also an important factor influencing the rate of saving. The more one is educated, the more one is in a position to realize the importance of savings, sooner or later, and accordingly, plans his family as well as family budget in a systematic manner.

Saving in the present study has been taken as a function of six socio-economic factors, viz., net income, asset level, age of chief earner, number of earners in the family, size of the family, level of education. Thus,

$$S = f(x_1, x_2, x_3, x_4, x_5, x_6) \quad ..(3.4)$$

Where S = Net saving including durables,

x_1 = Net income

x_2 = Asset

x_3 = Age of chief earner

x_4 = Number of earners in the family

x_5 = Size of family

x_6 = Education (average year of schooling)

We specify equation (3.4) above following semi-log function.

$$S = a+b_1 \log x_1 + b_2 \log x_2 + b_3 \log x_3 + b_4 \log x_4 + b_5 \log x_5 + b_6 \log x_6$$

Estimated Saving Relations

Four regression equations have been estimated, one each for the three categories of cultivator households, viz., large, medium and small, and the fourth one for the aggregate/total households. The estimated co-efficients, their associated 't' values and R^2 have been presented in Table 3.18.

Table 3.18 reveals that among the various factors which determine the level of savings, income (x_1) and

Table 3.18
Estimated Saving Relations

Type of Farmers	Constant (a)	x_1	x_2	x_3	x_4	x_5	x_6	R^2
Large Farmers	-147888.43	.2769*	.1689**	.0590*	.1963*	-.1214*	.2166*	-.62
		(4.61289)	(2.09994)	(3.40921)	(2.99569)	(-3.17788)	(1.98642)	
Medium Farmers	-108662.50	.1911*	.1136**	-.0327*	.2678	-.2357***	.1235*	.74
		(2.67854)	(1.98562)	(-3.26958)	(.86945)	(-1.89234)	(2.62392)	
Small Farmers	-24977.74	.1013**	.0235	.0021***	.1389	-.2624**	.0012	.41
		(1.98624)	(.632142)	(1.72321)	(.86352)	(-2.36291)	(.92145)	
All Farmers	-136970.31	.3569*	.2676*	-.1927*	.2367*	-.1238***	.1624***	.63
		(4.29231)	(2.93274)	(-.83652)	(2.68952)	(-1.92347)	(1.73234)	

Note: Figures in parentheses indicate 't' values.
* indicates that regression coefficient is significant at 1 per cent level of significance.
** indicates that regression coefficient is significant at 5 per cent level of significance.
*** indicates that regression coefficient is significant at 10 per cent level of significance.

assets (x_2), come out as the major determinants significantly and positively contributing to the savings in all the categories of cultivator households taken separately and together. There is no doubt, savings whether in the form of financial assets or physical assets or taken as aggregate of both, primarily depend on the level of income[8] and there is a direct function relationship between these two variables. It is hypothesized that since saving is determined by the level of per capita income, it must be negligible in low income countries. The most sophisticated reflection of this view can be found in celebrated (but of late debated) concept of vicious circle of poverty, that income is most important determinant of saving is not denied even by most adent supporter of the view that saving in the LDC's represents a respectable proportion of total output. However, it is hypothesized that income is only one (and not necessarily the most important) of the determinants of saving in the LDC's. Some studies even suggest that the association between saving and income, is, at best, tenuous[9].

Saving has been found to be negatively related to the age of the chief earner of the family (x_3) in the case of medium farmers and all farmers taken together, and positively related in the case of large and small farmers. Saving has been found to be negatively related to the size of family (x_5). Evidently the increasing ratio of dependents to total family members depletes the saving capacity of a household. Since the aged in general save less as they have already reached the peak earnings of their lives, a family, or economy, which supports a higher proportion of old and retired people will tend to save less or have a lower level of household savings.

Education level (x_6) of the chief earner has been found to be positively influencing the level of savings in all the categories of cultivator households. The relationship between education and savings has also been estimated by the NCAER (1980) Survey, which showed that with an education upto the middle class the average propensity to save was 15 per cent whereas it was 29 per cent in the case of graduates. Education is fundamentally concerned with the enhancement of quality of life in the sense that in whatever way quality of life is defined, education is a potential input into its attainment at the level both of the individual and the society at large. Admittedly, quality of life is a relative concept, signifying different things to different people, but there is no denying the fact that while divergencies exist, a substantial measure of consumers also exists about some of the major elements that go to contribute to quality of life.

As family participation in economic activity was a special feature of the rural economy, family labourers were treated as earners in this study and income for family labour engaged in capital formation was imputed and added to the household income. So, number of earners shows the positive relationship with savings. As the number of earner increases, saving also increases - saving coefficient is positive in the case of number of earners.

The explanatory variables considered here explain between 41 per cent to 74 per cent of the variations in savings. The intercept has been found to be negative for all the categories of cultivator households. This implies that dis-savings take place at zero level of disposable income which is consistent with the Keynesian concept of short-run consumption function.

The analysis of the major determinants of savings makes it clear that some of the factors pull it in a positive direction while the others pull it in a negative one. There is an aptitude to save among the cultivators either because they are more oriented to wealth accumulation or they prefer to abstain from luxurious and sophisticated consumption or they are conscious of their old age requirements.

Average and Marginal Rate of Saving

Keynes treated saving as a function of current income. As income increases, saving increases and incremental saving is more than proportional to the incremental income. The Keynesian hypothesis, as such implies that :

(i) average propensity to save (APS) is less than the marginal propensity to save (MPS), and

(ii) the average propensity to save (APS) increases with income.

The hypothesis did not receive consistent support from the various empirical studies. The cross section studies confirmed the Keynesian position while the time-series studies refuted it. As a result, economists got interested into explaining and reconciling the conflicting evidence and many theories and explanations have since been given.

In spite of the emergence of these theories, current income as a determinant of current savings has remained an accepted fact. Among the relatively more important studies, Kuznets (1960) found a positive correlation between per capita income and the ratio of personal saving to personal disposable income for both the developed and the developing countries. Most of the studies pertaining to the Indian economy have upheld the Keynesian hypothesis. The survey conducted by the NCAER (1980) has revealed a household saving ratio increasing with the income level. The evidence gathered by the present study also supports the Keynesian hypothesis.

The lower marginal rate of saving in the case of small farmers as compared to that in the case of the medium and large farmers at all the income levels, lends support to the wealth theories of consumption. It is a common experience that a rich agriculturist would normally have a lower saving propensity than a rich businessman. A possible explanation of this phenoenon may be the feeling of a greater security in land ownership than in the ownership of business assets. Another could be the socio-economic milien in whcih they respectively live. Yet another could be the greater opportunity in the latter case to channelize potential saving into actual saving in the form of financial and/or physical assets. The experience of Japan also shows that the rate of saving is the lowest among the farm households and the highest among the non-farm business proprietor households. It would be interesting to see how our estimates of the saving propensities for the rural sector in Haryana compare with those for the rural sector in India as a whole.

Our estimates of average and marginal propensities to save for cultivator households in Haryana are .29 and .36 respectively whereas for the rural India as a whole, according to the NCAER study (1980) the estimates of average and marginal propensities are .19 and .39 respectively. The behaviour of average propensity to save and marginal propensity to save, shows that while the former is higher for the state, the latter is lower than at the all-India level.

Attitude Towards and Motivations for Saving

Attitudes towards and motivations for saving are important factors in the determination of the propensity to save of different categories of households and the amounts saved by them. Data on the attitudinal aspect has been taken in this study mainly because the questions about the people's opinions and attitudes help establish a rapport with the respondents. Most people like to be asked about their opinion or their preferences or about their motives for savings. This is not so in the case of questions about amounts earned or saved. A good number of households do not like to disclose data. However, an insight into their attitudes about saving and motives/preference towards alternative saving outlets is of the great interest in its own right. For purposes of economic planning we need to know not only how much is saved by various groups/categories in the population but also how the saving preferences might be improved. A knowledge of saving motives can be useful in framing appeals to the population for a greater saving efforts. And understanding of saving preferences/motives can also be useful in designing saving instruments which effectively stimulate savings. (For instance, the saving instruments like National Saving Certificates, 'UTI' Master Shares, Indira Vikas Patras, etc. are intended to cater for the needs of people having different saving attitudes/motives).

Motivations for Saving

Various hypotheses have been postulated by economists regarding motives for savings. The 'normal income' hypotheses by Crockett and Friend and the 'life time income' hypotheses of Ando and Modigliani attract attention. The 'normal income' hypothesis explains that every household has a desired level of wealth which is accumulated over years. The desired level of wealth, which they term as normal wealth, depends upon income, household size and so on. If actual level of wealth is below the normal wealth, the household gets an inducement to save. The larger the difference, the larger is the propensity to save[10].

In India, particularly in the countryside, accumulation of wealth is synonymous with social prestige. It is generally observed that social prestige bears a positive relationship with the accumulated wealth. The more the wealth accumulated by a family, the greater its social prestige.

Another hypothesis is based on the notion of saving for old age, called 'hump saving'. Each individual saves during his active life span and dissaves during retirement.

This explains the term 'hump saving'. The individual saving pattern shows a 'hump' in the active life period. The 'life time income hypothesis expresses the similar opinion. This hypothesis of Modigliani and Ando postulates that individuals adopt a planning horizon for their life time consumption. They accumulate enough saving during their earning years to maintain their consumption standard during their non-earning old age[11].

Saving is not a mere non-spending, it represents a positive act involving deliberate decision making, a concious choice between present and future expectations. It entails a sacrifice or abstinence and obviously there must be strong motives which outweigh the temptation to spend it all.

We may presume that besides other factors such as education, age, family size and age of the head of the household, etc., source of income of household broadly indicates the household saving motives. Accordingly, for the analysis of the behaviour of saving motives we have classified all cultivator households into three categories, viz., large farmers, medium farmers and small farmers. The begin with, the possible motives for saving were classified into nine categories and were made known to the respondents. Each respondent was asked to indicate his relative importance of these motives for savings by assigning three preferences in decending order. The preferences of cultivator households for various motives have been shown in Table 3.19 through Table 3.21.

The tables reveal the following : In the case of large farmers 'saving for emergencies' was favoured by maximum number of households. As many as 21.07 per cent of the households gave first preference to this motive. The next most important motive for 18.67 per cent of the households was 'saving to enlarge business/farm activities'. The other motives which got significant number of first preferences are 'saving to build a house' (17.39 per cent), 'saving for dowaries, wedding and other social ceremonies'

Table 3.19
Percentage Distribution of Cultivator Households by Different Motives and Their Preferences (Large Farmers)

Motive for Saving		First Preference	Second Preference	Third Preference
I.	Saving for emergencies	21.07	10.35	10.08
II	Saving for old age	8.75	16.42	16.58
III.	Saving for dowaries, Wedding and other social ceremonies	13.72	8.73	10.69
IV.	Saving for gifts, donations and pilgrimage	2.43	6.75	6.06
V.	Saving to buy consumer durables	5.89	6.20	11.73
VI.	Saving to enlarge business/ farm activities	18.67	18.09	13.52
VII.	Saving for the education of the children	11.76	12.93	11.59
VIII.	Saving to build a house	17.39	18.10	15.32
IX.	Saving to help the Nation	0.32	2.43	4.43

Table 3.20
Percentage Distribution of Cultivator Households by Different Motives and Their Preferences (Medium Farmers)

Motive for Saving		First Preference	Second Preference	Third Preference
I.	Saving for emergencies	13.30	17.79	13.63
II.	Saving for old age	6.07	12.23	12.85
III.	Saving for dowaries, wedding and other social ceremonies	7.72	6.72	10.59
IV.	Saving for gifts, donations and pilgrimage	1.15	8.75	5.58
V.	Saving to buy consumer durables	4.38	8.32	14.06
VI.	Saving to enlarge business/ farm activities	24.16	16.72	16.80
VII.	Saving for the education of the children	19.72	12.89	8.86
VIII.	Saving to build a house	22.75	13.83	11.92
IX.	Saving to help the nation	0.75	2.75	5.71

Table 3.21
Percentage Distribution of Cultivator Households by Different Motives and Their Preferences (Small Farmers)

Motive for Saving	First Preference	Second Preference	Third Preference
I. Saving for emergencies	20.96	18.35	9.75
II. Saving for old age	14.07	16.09	8.29
III. Saving for dowaries, wedding and other	12.11	7.65	21.38
IV. Saving for gifts, donations and pilgrimage	1.58	4.09	14.89
V. Saving to buy consumer durables	6.19	12.78	9.84
VI. Saving to enlarge business/ farm activities	4.27	2.46	9.70
VII. Saving for the education of the children	18.08	15.97	8.70
VIII. Saving to build a house	20.85	19.72	12.95
IX. Saving to help the nation	1.39	2.89	4.50

(13.72 per cent), 'saving for the education of children' (11.76 per cent) and 'saving for old age' (Rs. 8.75 per cent). 'Saving to build a house' got the highest number of responses for second preference and the 'saving for old age' got the highest percentage figure for third preference.

In the case of medium farm households 'saving to enlarge business/farm activities' got the first preference for maximum number of households (24.16 per cent). Other motives which got the significant number of first preference are 'saving to build a house' (22.75 per cent), 'saving for the education of the children' (19.72 per cent), and 'saving for emergencies' (13.30 per cent). The highest number of households gave 'saving for emergencies' (17.79 per cent), and 'saving to enlarge business farm activities' (16.80 per cent) as the second and third preferences respectively.

For small farm households, the most important motive for saving is 'emergencies'. As many as 20.85 per cent households gave first preference to this motive. Other important motives for saving for this category are 'saving to build a house' (20.96 per cent), 'saving for education of the children' (18.08 per cent), 'saving for old age' (14.07 per cent) and 'saving for dowaries, wedding and other social ceremonies' (12.11 per cent). For second and third preferences, 'saving to build a house' and 'saving for dowaries, wedding and social ceremonies' got the top priority, being 19.72 per cent and 21.38 per cent, respectively.

As may be seen from Table 3.22, for all categories of cultivator households taken together, 'saving to build a house' was favoured by the maximum number of households (20.36 per cent) followed by 'saving for emergencies' (18.41 per cent) and 'saving for the education of children' (16.52 per cent). 'Saving to build a house' got the highest number of responses for second preference

Table 3.22
Distribution of Cultivator Households by Different Motives and Their Preferences (All Farmers)

Motive for Saving		First Preference	Second Preference	Third Preference
I.	Saving for emergencies	18.41	15.50	11.15
II.	Saving for old age	9.63	14.91	12.57
III.	Saving for dowaries, wedding and other social ceremonies	11.18	7.70	14.22
IV.	Saving for gifts, donations and pilgrimage	1.72	6.53	8.84
V.	Saving to buy consumer durables	5.50	9.10	11.88
VI.	Saving to enlarge business/farm/ activities	15.70	12.42	13.34
VII.	Saving for the education of the children	16.52	13.93	9.72
VIII.	Saving to build a house	20.36	17.22	13.40
IX.	Saving to help the nation	0.98	2.69	4.88

and 'saving for dowaries, wedding and other social ceremonies got the maximum responses for the third preferences.

Undoubtedly, the strength of motives for saving varies from one category of cultivator households to another. For instance, while the motive of 'saving for emergencies', got the most important place in the case of large farmers, it is 'saving to enlarge business/farm activities' in the case of medium farmers and 'saving for the education of children' in the case of small farmers. Even then the data on motives for saving are important, for they not only show a very wide spread tendency to save but awareness among all population groups of specific reasons why saving is advantageous. This might help the government to make use of these motives in order to stimulate more wide spread schemes to promote small savings. Suitable policies aiming at optimum exploitation of households resources can be framed to accelerate the saving propensities.

References

1. N.C.A.E.R. *Income Saving and Investment in Rural Sectors: A Study of Western U.P., Haryana and Punjab*, New Delhi, 1983.

2. Investment is taken here both in physical and financial assets. Physical investment relates to the real investment in the economy which is also known as capital formation. The U.N. Paper on capital formation defines net capital formation as additions to fixed capital and working capital available for future production, after allowances are made for depreciation, obsolescence and accidental damage to the fixed capital. (Concepts and Definitions of Capital Formation, Statistical Office of the United Nations, July, 1953, p. 7, Quoted from the AIR CS Report, 1950-51 (Published in 1956, p. 709).

3. Lydall (1953), p. 137.

4. Duesenberry (1967), p. 27.

5. For instance studies conducted by NCAER, RBI, CSO, and individuals.

6. Gupta (1972), p. 471.

7. A direct relationship between high birth rate and dependency ratio and its negataive impact on saving rate has been confirmed in a case study of 47 less developed countries see, Leff (1969).

8. Keynes, J.M., *The General Theory of Employment, Interest and Money*, Macmillan and Company,London, 1964, p. 97.

9. Kuznets, Simon, "Quantitative Aspects of Economic Growth–Long Term Trend in Capital Formation Proportions" *Economic Development and Cultural Change*, Vol. IX. July 1961, p.7.

10. Crockett J. and I. Friend, *Consumer Investment Behaviour in Determinants of Investment Behaviour*, NBER, Princeton, 1967.

11. Modigliani, F. and A. Ando, "The Life Cycle Hypothesis Saving; Aggregate Implications and Tests", *American Economic Review*, LIII (1963), pp. 55-84.

4

Conclusions

In this chapter, we shall try to put together some of the more interesting of the behaviour relationships and make some suggestions and concluding observations. The study has attempted an analysis of the structure and relationship as pertain to income, assets, savings, investment, etc. of agricultural households in Haryana. The analysis has been based on the primary data collected from a sample of 320 cultivator households for the crop year 1989-90.

As is well-known, the Haryana economy is primarily an agricultural economy with nearly 80 per cent of the state's population being employed directly or indirectly in agriculture and with more than 50 per cent of the state domestic product being generated in this sector of the economy. As a result of the technological break-through and the efforts made by the state government in buildiing up the infrastructure facilities, the agricultural sector of the state economy started generating additional income and its status in terms of per capita income improved rapidly. The average income of the cultivator households has shown an average increase of 11.39 per cent per annum over the period 1966-90. In view of the predominant role of agriculture in the state economy, it is important and of interest to analyse the various causes and consequences of the development process in relation to this sector. In the present study, we have focussed upon the income and asset structure and saving investment behaviour of cultivator households in the state. This among other things, would help up to evaluate how agricultural sector of the state economy has been affected by the general growth process and how, more importantly, has it in turn affected the overall growth process. As stated earlier, the study covered a sample of 320 cultivator households. These were taken from four different districts of the state. The sample households have been divided into three categories: small, medium and large comprising 71 large, 66 medium and 183 small cultivator households or farmers. This is representative of the overall size and composition of cultivator households in the state.

Our analysis is based on cross section data, the relevant data on time series being not available. Reliability of data depends on the skill efficiency and preservance of the interviewers and appropriateness of the format and contents of the questionaire from the point of view of relevance, managability and feasibility. The respondents in may cases have been found to have had a feeling of fear and suspicious or indifference while giving necessary information. This is true of the people anywhere in India but it is more so of people in rural parts who are mostly illiterate and not used in such encounters.

Secondly, treatment of depreciation at a uniform rate, the question of longevity of the assets and current valuation of assets cannot be said to be free from some degree of arbitrariness. Lastly, the use of some of the quantitative techniques has been made. The important quantitative techniques used in the study are : concentration ratio, standard deviation of logarithms, coefficient of variation, and Theil Index.

Income Composition and Distribution

The sources of income of cultivator households have been classified under the following main heads:

(i)agriculture, (ii) livestock, (iii) agricultural and

non-agricultural wages, (iv) business, crafts and professions, (v) salaries, (vi) rental income from housing, etc. (vii) interests and dividents and pensions, (viii) current transfers, and (ix) any others.

The data on various components of income in respect of different categories of cultivator households reveal that in the case of large farmers, agriculture constitutes the single most important component of household income, contributing 64.13 per cent of the total household income of this category, followed by livestock and interests, dividends and pensions, and others with 24.01 per cent and 4.00 per cent, respectively. All other components are relatively less significant. In the case of medium farmers, agriculture contributes 43.74 per cent of the total household income of this category, followed, again, by livestock and interest, dividends and pensions, and others with 32.78 per cent and 8.82 per cent shares, respectively. Interestingly in this category also, all other components are relatively less significant. Thus, almost the same pattern emerges in both the categories of households, i.e., large and medium, except that agricultural income has a relatively higher proportion in the case of the large category whereas livestock income has a relatively higher share in the case of the medium category.

In the case of small farmers, agriculture and livestock are the two important components and constitute 35.51 and 33.62 per cent shares, respectively, both having more or less equal importance in this category. Salaries and business, crafts and professions account for 12.60 per cent and 8.74 per cent respectively. The contribution of the remaining sources in this category is rather insignificant.

So far as the cultivator households as a whole are concerned, nearly 49 per cent of the income is generated from agriculture followed by 29.39 per cent from livestock, 7.54 per cent from salaries and 5.09 per cent from business, crafts and professions. Contribution made by wage is just 1.06 per cent. If we look at the category-wise break-up of the total income of households, we find that large farmers occupy the most predominant place with 42.15 per cent share in the total income followed by small farmers (36.61 per cent). Medium farmers occupy the third place with only 21.24 per cent share in the total income (Table 2.1).

A similar pattern emerges in all the categories of households, i.e., large, medium and small, in the sense that nearly more than 70 per cent of the income is generated from agriculture and livestock. It is, however, interesting to note that while the percentage share of income from agriculture declines when we move from large to medium to small farmers categories, the behaviour of income generated from livestock shows just the reverse picture, i.e., its share increases when we move from large to medium to the small farmers.

As regards income inequality (Table 2.2) the cultivator households have been divided into three categories, lower income group (upto Rs. 30000), middle income group (Rs. 30001 to Rs. 70000) and large income group (above Rs. 70,000). In the case of both small and medium farmers, percentage share of income increases as we move from lower income group to middle income group and decreases as we move to higher income group of cultivator households, i.e. 44.34 per cent to 52.58 per cent, and 8.04 per cent to 71.23 per cent and decreases to 3.08 per cent and 20.73 per cent respectively. But in the case of large farmers, the percentage share of income has been found to be increasing as we move from lower income group to middle and then to higher income group with a share of 0.46 per cent to 22.83 per cent to 76.71 per cent respectively. Taken together, the percentage share of income is increasing from lower income group of middle income group and decreasing from middle to higher income group i.e., from 18.13 per cent to 44 per cent to 37.87 per cent, respectively.

There is considerable inequality in the distribution of income both within and among different categories of cultivator households. Income is more evenly distributed in the case of the small and medium farmers, as compared to large farmers and the cultivator households taken together.

The value of Gini ratio as an index/measure of income inequality has been found to be 0.232, 0.135 and 0.242, in the case of small, medium and large farmers, respectively (Table 2.4). The values of the concentration ratio shows that there is no consistent relation between the size of the holdings and degree of intra-size equality of income distribution. Thus, the income is almost equally evenly distributed in the case of the small and the large farmers, whereas it is relatively more evenly distributed in the case of medium farmers as compared to large and small farmers. The measures of inequality such as the co-efficient of variation of income and the standard deviation of logarithms of income also confirm this pattern. However, the Thiel Index gives a slightly differnt pattern of income inequality.

Asset Structure and Distribution

In their approaches to consumption function, economists like Friedman (1957), Modigliani (1963), Spiro (1962), and Clower and Johnson (1968) have widely recognised the role of assets as one of the determinants of household saving. Thus there are reasons for supposing that asset structure play some significant role. The volume and character of the assets which the households possess at any point in time is likely to condition their desire to accumulate more.

Assets have been divided into two categories:

(i) physical assets and (ii) financial assets.

Physical assets include land (including vacant house sites) buildings (residental and other property), cattle sheds, farm buildings, livestock, agricultural implements and machinery (including means of irrigation), business assets (including business permises, means of transport and other nonfarming machinery) and consumer durables. Financial assets consist of amount deposited with the bank/post offices, premium paid to life insurance corporation, provident fund contributions, shares (of cooperative bank/societies, cooperative mills, etc.) and gold and jewellery. So far as the values of these assets are concerned, it is mainly based on the information supplied by respondents during the reference period.

The asset structure of the cultivator households in terms of percentage shares (Table 2.9) indicates that land dominates the total assets with a share of 78.46 per cent. Next in importance are buildings with a share of 7.58 per cent, followed by agricultural implements and machinery (4.74 per cent) and live-stock (with a share of 3.09 per cent). The other assets account for a very small fraction of the total. Significantly, a large chunk of total assets of households is in the form of physical assets accounting for as much as 97.08 per cent. The financial assets, on the other hand, just account for the remaining 2.92 per cent. The possible reason for such a behaviour would seem to be that the physical assets, especially land, are acquired and retained mainly as a source of higher agricultural output and partly due to having a higher level of social status among the farming community. Financial assets, on the other hand, are mainly acquired as a provision for a time of need and sometimes to be used as working capital, although exceptionally. Financially assets are generally kept inthe form of precious metals by the cultivator households and sometimes used as security for procuring loans especially from money-lenders. These may, therefore, be considered as a potential source, though a limited one, to be drawn upon for investment. Even if some margin for under-estimation and concealment is allowed, it would be little significance.

The asset structure varies across the three categories

of cultivator households. Although land dominates the total assets in the case of all categories of households taken separately and together, their percentage shares varies significantly. For example, in the case of large farmers, land accounts for 81.68 per cent, while the percentage share of this asset is 78.63 per cent and 71.71 per cent in the case of medium farmers and small farmers, respectively. Among the large and medium farmers buildings, implements and machinery and financial assets are other major assets, accounting for 5.41 per cent, 5.23 per cent, 2.83 per cent and 7.45 per cent, 5.45 per cent, 3.01 per cent, respectively. Buildings, livestock, and implements and machinery account for 12.12 per cent, 4.92 per cent and 4.01 per cent shares, respectively, of the total assets among the small farmers.

In order to examine the asset distribution, the cultivator households in each size category have been classified by the level of asset holding. In all, thirteen asset-levels have been conceived, with assets worth upto Rs. 5,00,000 constituting the lowest asset-level and assets valuing more than Rs.20,00,000 constituting the highest asset-level. Table 2.2 presents the pattern of asset distribution emerging from this grouping. In the case of large farmers, 2.82 per cent of the total cultivator households fall in the lowest asset class and they account for only 0.71 per cent of the total assets, while 21.13 per cent, the maximum proportion in any category, falls in the Rs. 10,00,001 - 15,00,000 asset-group and account for 18.19 per cent of total assets. 14.08 per cent households in this category fall in the highest asset-group and account for a 35.87 per cent of the total assets held by the category (large farmers) as a whole.

Among the medium farmers, 36.36 per cent households fall in the lowest asset-group (upto Rs. 5,00,000) with a 23.30 per cent share in the total assets of the category, while 28.79 per cent households fall in the Rs. 5,00,001 - 6,00,000 asset group and account for 24.19 per cent of the total assets. Only 1.52 per cent households in this category fall in the highest asset-group with a share of 4.99 per cent in the total assets.

In the case of small farmers, 93.45 per cent, the highest proportion in any size category, fall in the lowest asset-group and account for the bulk, i.e., 81.73 per cent, of the total assets of this category. Interestingly, but not unexpectedly, not even a single household in this category falls in the highest asset-group.

For all the households taken together, 61.57 per cent fall in the lower asset-group accounting for 26.42 per cent of the total assets, while 3.43 per cent households fall in the highest asset-group accounting for 19.79 per cent of the total assets.

Top 10 per cent of the cultivator households in Haryana hold about 37 per cent i.e. about two fifths, of the total assets, while bottom 10 per cent hold a mere 2 per cent (Table 2.11). Categorywise, the top 10 per cent account for 26 per cent of the total assets in the case of the large farmers, 16 per cent in the case of medium farmers and 21 per cent in the case of small farmers. In contrast, the shares of bottom 10 per cent in the total assets of respective categories are only 4.56 per cent, 6.97 per cent and 4.23 per cent.

The relative position of the top 20 per cent of the large farmers on the asset scale is superior to their counterparts in the other size categories. But the bottom 80 per cent of the large farmers are worse off as compared to the other categories in this respect. The concentration ratio, co-efficient of variation and standard deviation of logarithms, also confirm the above results.

The above analysis enables us to conclude that there exists a large scale disparities in terms of asset holding among the cultivator households taken together, in general, and the large farmers taken separately, in particular.

Investment Composition and Distribution

There has been significant variations in the volume and composition of gross investment across the different categories of cultivator households. Large farmers' share in total gross investment has been found to be the highest (51.33 per cent) and that of medium farmers the lowest (20.06 per cent). Small farmers' share in total gross investment accounted for a higher percentage in comparison to that of the medium farmers (Table 3.1). The share of physical investment in total investment is higher (28.57 per cent) in the case of large farmers in comparison to medium (10.79 per cent) and small farmers (20.76 per cent). Thus, the medium farmers again have the lowest share in this respect. The share of financial investment in total investment is also higher (22.76 per cent) in the case of large farmers compared to medium (9.23 per cent) and small farmers (7.85 per cent). In the case of financial investment, the relative importance of medium farmers is higher than that of the small farmers which is not the case relating to the physical investment.

So far as the composition of net investment (physical and financial taken together) is concerned, the proportion of net investment to total net investment is found to be the highest (52.46 per cent) in the case of large farmers and the lowest (19.40 per cent) in the case of medium farmers. The proportion of net physical investment to total household investment is 21.65 per cent in the case of large farmers followed by 17.51 per cent in the case of small and 6.84 per cent for medium farmers. The share of net financial investment is higher in the case of large and medium farmers, being 30.82 per cent and 12.56 per cent, respectively, as compared to the small farmers (10.62 per cent). (Table 3.2).

For all the households taken together, the financial investment constitutes 46 per cent and physical investment 54 per cent of the total assets. It has been found that the investible surplus is channelized by the cultivator households in Haryana mainly into three categories, i.e. livestock, agricultural implements and machinery, and buildings. Investment in agricultural implements and machinery which accounts for 24.79 per cent of the total physical investment could be said to be an indication of the extent to which modernisation and mechanisation is taking place in Haryana agriculture. Buildings also account for almost a similar proportion, 24.48 per cent, of total physical investment. But above all the investment in live-stock attracts the largest proportion, as much as 26.22 per cent, of the total physical investment, which reflects that this asset continues to occupy its importance in the agriculture sector of the state. The shares of land, consumer durables, farm houses and cattle sheds, and business assets come next in order in this respect.

Categorywise, agricultural implements and machinery, buildings and land are of higher importance than other components of physical investment, in the case of large farmers, while in the case of medium farmers, livestock (5.04 per cent), agricultural implements and machinery (4.65 per cent) and land (4.56 per cent) are the three important components having precedence over other components. In the case of small farmers, livestock, buildings, and agricultural implements and machinery are of higher importance among different components of physical investment being 13.38 per cent, 11.91 per cent and 7.18 per cent, respectively.

The composition of net financial investment of different categories of cultiator households, on the whole, shows that the bank deposits account for as high as 78.58 per cent, the highest of the total net investment followed by gold and jewellery (11.81 per cent). The percentage share of premium paid to the L.I.C. is relatively lower in almost all the categories. However, the investment in small savings by the large farmers (3.47 per cent) is relatively higher (Table 3.4).

The relationship between investment and some of

the selected socio-economic factors, such as income, asset, age of the chief earner, number of earners, size of the family and education level of the chief earners has been depicted in Table 3.14. Among the various factors which determine the level of investment, income comes out as one of the major determinants positively contributing to investment for all categories of cultivator households. Investment has been found to be negatively related to the age of the chief earner in all categories except the medium farmers, and to the size of the family for all categories. Investment has a positive relationship with asset level•in all categories except the small farmers. Education level of the chief earner and the number of earners also have a positive relationship to investment for all categories of cultivator households taken separately and together.

The explanatory variables considered here explain 38 per cent to 74 per cent of the variations in investment. The intercept has been found to be positive for all categories of cultivator households. This implies that investment takes place even at zero level of disposable income which is consistent with the accepted principles. We know that a household makes investment from three sources, viz., current svings, past savings and borrowings. The households make investment in enlarging their activities by borrowing even through they have zero level of disposable income. It clearly brings out the healthy attitude of farmers in the state towards taking risk for capital formation.

Saving Composition and Distribution

Among the different categories of cultivator households. Large farmers contribute most of the total savings, gross as well as net. They save as much as 54.74 per cent of the gross savings and 57.96 per cent of the net savings. As against this, the shares of small farmers are 26.51 per cent and 24.84 per cent respectively. Saving of medium farmers (18.75 per cent gross and 17.20 per cent net) are lower in comparison to the other two categories (Table 3.15). The dominant position of the large farm households is mainly due to the fact that they enjoy disproportionately large shares in total assets, physical (47.51%) as well as financial (57.07 per cent).

Among the various factors which determine the level of savings, income has been found as one of the major determinants positively contributing to saving for all the three categories of cultivator households taken separately and together. Savings has been found to be negatively related to the age of chief earner and size of the family. It is believed that the larger the size of the family, the higher the income and resultant savings. However, we find that the increasing ratio of dependents to total family members results in low saving. Since the aged people in general save less as they have already reached or crossed the peak earnings of their lives, a country which supports a higher proportion of old and retired people will tend to save less or have a lower level of household savings. This is borne out by the fact that young people generally separate themselves and live in small families with the result that they spend a higher proportion of their income. Education level of the chief earner has been found to be positively influencing by the level of savings in all categories of cultivator households.

Even high income cannot take the form of saving unless there is an aptitude to save. Aptitude to save is guided, among other things, by desire to accumulate wealth. Wealth/assets has also been found to have a positive relationship with savings. The "number of earners" also shows a positive relationship with savings, as with the increasing number of earners the savings also tend to increase.

The explanataory variables considered here explain between 41 per cent and 74 per cent of the variations in savings. The intercept has been found to be negataive for all the categories of cultivator households, which implies that dissavings takes place at zero level of disposable income which can be said to be consistent with the Keynesian concept of short-run consumption function.

The above analysis of the behaviour of the major determinants of savings reveals that while some of the factors influence savings in a positive direction, others pull it in a negative one. The propensity to save and the saving behaviour of the cultivators is governed mainly by their inclination and bias towards wealth accumulation, their indifference towards, if not abstention from, conspicuous-luxurious consumption, and their urge to provide for the future requirements.

A lot of attention has been given to the problems of Indian rural sector by planners and policy makers, especially since the early seventies. Now a days, the prime concern of the Government is to reduce the inequalities of income and wealth so that the fruits of development do reach the last man, i.e., the poorest among the poor. To improve the economic well-being of the weaker section (like small and marginal farmers, agriculture labourers and to reduce the gap between haves and have nots, Government of India has launched various developmental programmes focussing on these sections of the society. Some of these programmes are Community Development Programme (1951-51), Intensive Agricultural Development Programme (1965), Small Farmers Development Agency (SFDA) and Marginal Farmers Development Agency (MFDA) (1969), etc.

Our analysis of the distribution of income and assets and of the saving and investment behaviour reveals that there are wide inequalities in the distribution of income and assets. On the one extreme are the large farmers who have substantial asset holdings, high incomes, high saving propensities, a luxurious life style and all facilities within their reach, and on the other extreme are the majority of small farmers whose assets continue to be meagare and unproductive, income insufficient to meet even the basic needs of life and limited access to welfare programmes. Large size of families, wide-spread illiteracy, and poor health and sanitary conditions continue to be typical of the poor. The authorities have initiated a lot of measures to ameliorate their conditions and succeeded to some extent and in some directions. The authorities seem, however, to have failed rather miserably in narrowing down the gap between the rich and the poor; particularly in making the rich to contribute their share to the state pool in return for the disproportionately large gains that they have reaped as a result of various rural welfare programmes.

The problem of inequality both in incomes and in assets is very stupendous and complex having wide social, economic and political ramification. It is not surprising that it has evaded solution for a period of over four decades under the kind of economic system India has opted for tackling the basic economic problems. While no doubt the issues of how much is produced and how fast, are crucial and important, the issues of what is produced and how it is distributed, have to be assigned the top priority. In other words, while the objective of growth is important, objective of growth with justice is far more important. A definite re-scheduling of priorities is called for.

Promotion of co-operative forms of production, elimination of functionless rent receivers, private usurious and monopoly, and enlargement of public sector in strategic lines of production and trade are of far reaching significance in achieving the equalitarian ideals. A ceiling on income is, in other words, the end point of a process; it cannot be beginning. It must raise incomes of the lowest levels and it must simultaneously reduce incomes of the top. The quicker the advance towards this pattern, the more rapidly will economic disparities disappear. The redistribution of incomes and assets will increase the saving potential of the cultivator households.

The study also calls for the implementation of family planning programmes with greater stress on restricting the family planning programmes with greater stress on restricting the family size. Large family size means more consumption and consequently low saving level. Many studies conducted in India and abroad by various scholars confirm the desirability of the implementation of family planning programmes as larger families have never been conducive to attain the higher standard of living and welfare of the society.

Another important implication of the study is that education has been found to be positively contributing to the saving behaviour of the cultivator households. But it has been found that most of the cultivator households covered by the present study are illiterate and do not plan their family budgets in an appropriate manner. National education programme should be implemented in rural areas so as to raise the level of education of the rural households, in general, and the cultivator households, in particular.

The investment pattern of the cultivator households revealed a traditional pattern as more than 60 per cent of the total savings of the cultivator households is channelised into the accumulation of physical assets alone. For the development of the economy as a whole, the financial investment is also equally, if not more, important. Most of the viable financial investments are either unknown to the cultivators or there is lack of sound financial agency to channelise their savings. Savings in the form of premia for life insurance schemes, deposits in savings banks, and postal savings including Kisan Vikas Patra, Indira Vikas Patra, etc., must be promoted by the concerned agencies in the interior parts of the rural areas. The schemes like crop-insurance and cattle insurance should be given special attention. This will mobilise substantial surplus from the cultivator households which can be ploughed back for agricultural development.

Bibliography

Ackely, Gardner, *Macro Economic Theory,* The Macmillan Company, New York, 1969.

Adam Smith, *An Enquiry into the Nature and Causes of Wealth of Nations,* Edwin Cannan and Co. Ltd., London, 1950.

Ahluwalia, M.S., "Rural Poverty and Agricultural Performance in Indian", *Journal of Development Studies,* April, 1978.

Ahmed, Syed, "The Saving-Wealth Relation and the Measure of the Real Value of Assets", *The Journal of Political Economy,* Vol. LXX, No. 3, June, 1962.

Alain, Anthoven, "The Growth of Investment Credit and Future of Prosperity", *The American Economic Review,* Vol. XLVII, No. 6, Dec., 1957.

Awasthi, D.S., (Ed.), "Income Saving and Capital Formation in Rural India", *Indian Economic Association,* 1984.

Atkinson, A.B., "Import Strategy and Growth Under Conditions of Stagnant Export Earning", *Oxford Economic Papers,* Vol. 21, Nov. 1969, pp. 325-28.

Atkinson, A.B., "On the Measurement of Inequalities", *Journal of Economic Theory,* Vol. 2, September, 1970.

Bahadur, Jagdish, L.S. Rathore, and R.K. Dutta, "Role of Agro Meteorology in Agricultural Development", *Yojna,* Vol. 34, No. 19, October 16-31, 1990.

Basu, Sreelekha, "Pattern of Asset Holdings in India—A Study of Top Asset Holders", *Economic and Political Weekly*, Vol. XI, No. 28, July 10, 1976.

Bhagwati, J & Chakaravarty, S., "Contributions to Indian Economic Analysis", *A Survey A.E.R.*, Vol. 59, Part-II, September, 1969, pp. 2-73.

Bhalla, Surjit, S., "The Role of Sources of Income and Investment Opportunities in Rural Savings", *Journal of Development Economics*, Vol. 5, No. 3.

Bhanja, Prasanta Kumar, "Capital Formation in Agriculture at the Farm Level", *Indian Journal of Agricultural Economics*, Vol. XX, No. 1, Jan.-March, 1965.

Bhaty, I.Z. and Sarma M.T.R., "Saving Behaviour in India and Implications for Policy", in C.D. Wadwa (Ed.) Some Problems of India's Economic Policy, *Tata McGraw Hill*, Delhi, 1980.

Chaudhry, Uma Datta Roy, Katyal, R.P. and Chatruvedi, B.N., "Pattern of Saving and Investment in India since 1950-51", *Margin*, Vol. 12, No. 1, October, 1979.

Chenery, H.B. et. at., *Redistribution with Growth*, Oxford University Press, London, 1974.

Chenery, H.B. and A.M. Strout, "Foreign Assistance and Economic Development", *AER*, Vol. 56, Part I, September, 1966, pp. 679-733.

Choudhury R.A. and Shama Gamkhar, *The Indian Economy and Its Performance Since Independance*, Oxford University Press, New Dehli, 1991.

Clark, Colin, *Conditions of Economic Progress*, Macmillan, London, 1957.

Clower, O.R. and M. Johnson, *Income, Wealth and Theory of Consumption, in value captial and Economic Growth; Papers in Honour of Sir John Hicks,* (Ed.) by *J.N. Wafe, Edinbug* University Press, 1968.

Crockett J. and I. Friend, "Consumer Investment Behaviour in Determinants of Investment Behaviour", NBER, *Princeton,* 1967.

Dahiya, L.N., "Assets Distribution Among Rural Households", *Eastern Economists,* February, 13, 1981.

Dale, W. Admans, "Mobilizing Household Savings through Rural Financial Markets", *Economic Development and Cultural Change,* Vol. 26, No. 3, April, 1978.

Debroy, B., "Income Inequality in East Europe", *Artha Vijnana,* Vol. XXVIII, No. 3, September, 1986.

Desai, Nitin, "Asset Structure of Indian Rural Households", *Indian Economic Review,* Oct., 1978, Vol. XIII (New Series), No. 2.

Dogra, Bharat, "Land Reforms: Issues and Solutions", *Yojna,* Vol. 33, No. 6, April 15, 1989.

Domar, E.D., "Capital Expansion Rate of Growth and Employment", *Econometrice,* Vol. 14, April 1964, pp. 137-47.

Domar, E.D., "Expansion and Employment", *American Economic Review,* 37, 34-35, March, 1947.

Douglas Paul, *Theory of Wages,* Macmillan, New York, 1934.

Duesenberry, J.S., "*The Income Saving and Theory of Consumer Behaviour*", A Galaxy Book, Oxford University Press, 1967.

Friedman, Milton, *A Theory of the Consumption Function, A Study by the NBER,* New York, Number 63, General Series, Princeton University Press, 1957.

Friend, Irwin, "Individual's Saving—Volume and Composition", John Wiley and Sons, Inc., New York, *Chapman and Hall Limited,* London, 1954.

Fulcher, G.S., "Savings of Individuals in Relation to Income", *American Economic Review*, Vol. XXXII, 1942.

Gilbert, M., "Measuring National Income as Affected by War", *Journal of American Statistical Association*, Vol. XXXVII, 1942.

Gini, C., "Measurement of Inequality of Income", *Economic Journal*, Vo. 31, pp. 12, 3-12, 1931.

Goldsmith, R.W., *A Study of Saving in the United States*, Princeton University Press, Princeton, 1955.

Goldsmith, R.W., "The Volume and Components of Saving in the United States", *Studies in Income and Wealth*, Vol. III, N.B.E.R., New York, 1939.

Gupta, Kanhaya, L., "Dependency Rates and Saving Rates", *The American Economic Review*, June, 1971.

Gupta, K.L., "On Some Determinants of Rural and Urban Household Saving Behaviour", *Economic Record*, Vol. 46, 1970.

Harrod, R.F., *Towards a Dynamic Economics*, Macmillan, London, 1956.

Harrod, R.F., "An Essay in Dynamic Theory", *Economic Journal*, Vol. 49, June 1939, pp. 14-33.

Higgins, Benjamin, *Economic Development*, University Book Stall, New Delhi, 1990.

Higgins, Benjamin, *Final Report to the Govt. of the Philippines*, New York, 1957.

Johnson, D.W. and Chice, J., "The Saving Income Relation in Under Developed Countries", *Economic Journal*, Vol. LXXVIII, June, 1968.

Joshi, V., "Foreign Exchange Bottleneck or Unwillingness to Save", *Economic and Political Weekly*, Vol. 2, March, 1967, pp. 485-86.

Keynes, J.M., *The General Theory of Employment, Interest and Money,* Harcourt Brace and Company, New York, 1936.

Khare, M.P., "Income, Saving and Investment in Agriculturally Progressive Areas in Ahmednagar District, Maharastra State (1969-70 to 1971-72)", *Artha Vijnana,* Vol. XVII, No. 4, December, 1976.

Kakwani, N.C., *Income Inequality and Poverty,* Oxford University Press, New Delhi, 1980.

Klein, L.R., *An Introduction to Econometrics,* Prentice Hall of India (Pvt.) Ltd., New Delhi, 1965.

Kravis, I.B., *The Structure of Income,* University of Pensylvania, 1962.

Kuznets, Simon, "Quantitative Aspects of Economic Growth—Long Term Trend in Captial Formation Proportions", *Economic Development and Cultural Change,* Vol. IX, July, 1961.

Kuznets, Simon, *Income and Wealth of the Limited States,* Trends and Structures, Bowes and Bowes, London, 1952.

Kuznets, Simon, *Population Change and Aggregate Output in Demographic Change in Developing Countries.* Princeton, N.J., Princeton University Press, 1960.

Kuznets, Simon, *Modern Economic Growth,* Yale University Press, U.S.A., 1966.

Kuznets, Simon, *Economic Growth and Structure,* Oxford and IBH Publishing Co., Bombay, 1965.

Lahiri, A.K., "Asset Structure of Indian Rural Households", *Indian Economic Review,* Vol. 13, No. 2, (New Series), October, 1978.

Lawrence, S.K., "Resource Mobilization in India", *Yojna,* Vol. 31, No. 3, February, 16-28, 1987.

Leff, N.H., "Marginal Saving Rates in Development Process—The Brazilian Experience, *Economic Journal*, Vol. 28, 1968.

Lerner, Abba, T., "Saving and Investment, Definitions", *Margin*, Vol. 8, No. 2, August, 1969.

Leontief, W.W. and Others, *Studies in the Structure of American Economy*, Oxford, New York, 1953.

Lewis, W.A., *Economic Development with Unlimited Supplies of Labour*, Manchester School of Economic and Social Studies, No. 2, May 1854, Nurkse R. op. cit.

Lewis, W.A., *The Theory of Economic Growth*, Homewood III, 1955.

Lockwoord W.W., The Economic Development of Japan, Princeton, N.J., 1954.

Loknathan, P.S., *Pattern of Income Distribution and Saving*, Oxford Books and Stationary, New Delhi, 1967.

Lorenz, M.O., "Methods of Measuring and Concentration of Wealth", *Jounral of American Statistical Association*, Vol. 9, pp. 209-19, 1905.

Lydall, H.F., "This Inequality of Indian Incomes", *Economic Weekly*, Special Number, June, 1960.

Mahajan, O.P., "Economic Growth and Income Distribution in India: Trends, Prospects and Policy Implications", *The Indian Economic Journal*, Oct., Dec., 1977, Vol. 25, No. 2.

Mathur, J.S., *Measurement and Analysis of Saving*, Oxford Book and Stationary Company, Scindia House, New Delhi, 1962.

Meir, Geralds, *Leading Issues in Development Economics*, Oxford University Press, New York, 1964.

Meier, G.M. and Baldwin, R.E., *Economic Development*, Wiely, New York, 1957.

Mitra, P.K., *Aggregate Savings of Indian Economy,* Ajanta Publications, Delhi, 1987.

Modigliani, F. and A. Ando, "The Life-Cycle Hypothesis of Saving: Aggregate Implications and Tests", *American Economic Review,* Vol. III, 1963.

Nair, K. Ramchandran, "Capital Growth in Indian Agriculture", *Indian Journal of Agricultural Economics,* Vol. XX, No. 1, Jan-March, 1965.

Nagar, A.L. and R.K. Dass, *Basic Statistics,* Oxford University Press, New Delhi, 1977.

Narayana, D.L., *Income, Saving and Investment of Household Sector in Chittor District,* S. Chand and Company Ltd., New Delhi, 1979.

National Bureau of Economic Research, *Capital Formation and Economic Growth,* Princeton University Press, 1955.

N.C.A.E.R., *All Indian Household Survey of Income, Saving and Consumer Expenditure* (with special reference to 1970-71, New Delhi, 1975.

N.C.A.E.R., *Household Income and its Disposition,* New Delhi, 1980.

N.C.A.E.R., *Attitude Towards and Motives for Saving,* New Delhi, July, 1964.

N.C.A.E.R., *Income, Saving and Investment in Rural Sectors: A Study of Western U.P., Haryana and Punjab,* New Delhi, 1983.

Nelson, R.R., "The Effective Exchange Rate, Employment and Growth in a Foreign Exchange Constrained Economy", *Journal of Political Economy,* Vol. 78, May-June, 1970, pp. 546-64.

Nurkse, Ragnar, "Some International Aspects of the Problem of Economic Development", *American Economic Review,* Vol. 42, May 1952, pp. 571-83.

Nurkse, Ragnar, *Problems of Capital Formation*, Oxford University Press, New York, July, 1952.

Pandit, B.L., *The Growth and Structure of Savings in India*, Oxford University Press, New Delhi, 1991.

Panikar, P.G.K., *Rural Savings in India*, Somaiya Publication, Private Ltd., Bombay, July 1970.

Panikar, P.G.K., "Capital Formation in Indian Agriculture", *Indian Journal of Agricultural Economics*, Vol. XXIV, No. 4, Oct.-Dec., 1969.

Patel, I.J., "Saving, Investment and Economic Growth—A dynamic Approach", *Indian Economic Review*, August, 1959.

Paul Sweezy, *Theory of Capitalist Development*, Oxford University Press, New York, 1942.

Polak J.J., *The National Income of the Netherlands Indies*, 1921-1939, New York.

Raj, K.N., "The Marginal Rate of Savings in the Indian Economy", *Oxford Economic Papers*, 1961.

Ramesh, D. and Bhatnagar, D.S., "Agricultural Productivity in India—Study of its Directions and Dimensions in a Recent Octards", *The Indian Journal of Economics*, Oct., 1968, Vol. XLIX, No. 193.

Rao, K.S., *Papers on National Income and Allied Topics*, Vol. 1, Asia Publishing House, Bombay, 1960.

Rao, Sudha V., "Population and Development", *Margin*, Vol. 24, No. 2, Jan-March, 1992.

Rao, V.K.R.V., "Savings, Captial Formation and National Income", *Economic and Political Weekly*, Volume XV, No. 22, May 31, 1980.

Reddy, T. Prabhakar, "Agricultural Credit: A Study", *Yojna*, Vol. 34, No. 17, Sept. 16-30, 1990.

R.B.I., *All India Rural Credit Survey 1950-51,* "Concepts and Definitions of Capital Formation", Statistical Office of the United Nations, July, 1953.

Ricardo, David, *The Principles of Political Economy and Taxation,* Everyman's Library, London, 1912.

Robinson, Joan, *The Accumulation of Capital,* Macmillan, London, 1956.

Rosenstein Rodan, "Problem of Industrialisation of Eastern and South Eastern Europe", *The Econmic Journal,* Vol. 53, June-Sept. 1943, pp. 202-11.

Sahni, B.S., *Saving and Economic Development with Special Refernece to India,* Scientific Book Agency, Calcutta, 1967.

Sarma, I.R.K., "Changes in the Structure of Personal Saving", *Margin,* Vol. XI, No. 4, July, 1979.

Sarma, I.R.K., "Saving Behaviour of Household Sector", *Margin,* Vol. 12, No. 1, October, 1979.

Sarma, I.R.K., "Household Saving in Share and Securities", *Margin,* Vol. 12, No. 12, 1979.

Sen, A.K., "On Optimizing the Rate of Savings", *Economic Journal,* Sept., 1961.

Sen, A.K. and Raj, "Alternative Pattern of Growth under Conditions of Stagnant Export Earnings", *Oxford Economic Papers,* Vol. 13, Feb., 1961, pp. 43-52.

Schumpeter, J.A., *Business Cycles,* Vol. 1, First Edition, McGraw Hill, USA, 1939.

Shukla, Tara, *Capital Formation in Indian Agriculture,* Vora and Company, Bombay, 1956.

Singh, A.S. and Gurpreet, "Saving Behaviour of Cultivators in India with special reference to Punjab State", *Economic Affairs,* Vol. 31, No. 4, Dec., 1986.

Sinha, M.R., *Saving in the Economic Growth of Post-war, Japan,* Indian Institute of Asian Studies, Bombay, 1964.

Spiro, Alan, "Wealth and Consumption Function", *Journal of Political Economy,* Vol. LXX, No. 4, August, 1962.

Steward and Streeton, P., "New Strategy for Development: Poverty Income Distribution and Growth", *Oxford Economic Papers,* New Series, November, 1976, Vol. 28, No. 3.

Vashistha, Prem, "Income Wealth and Saving Suvey for Econometric Application", *Margin,* Vol. 14, No. 3, July, 1982.

Venkataramanan, L.S. & Prahaladachar, M., "Study of Cropping Pattern Changes in Andhra Pradesh During 1950-75", *Indian Economic Review,* October, 1978, XIII, (New Series) No. 2.

Wadhva, Charan, D., *Some Problems of India's Economy Policy,* Tata McGraw Hill Publishing Company Limited, New Delhi, 1980.

World Bank, "Determinants of Aggregate Savings", *I.B.R.D. Working Papers,* Allied Publishers Pvt. Ltd., Bombay, June, 1977.

World Bank, "The Role of Contractual Savings in Mobilization of Savings", *I.B.R.D. Working Papers,* Allied Publishers Private Ltd., Bombay, June, 1977.

Appendix I

Distribution of Cultivator Households by Income Level (Decile)

(Amount in Rs.)

Income Decile	Large Farmers	Medium Farmers	Small Farmers
Ist Decile	262621 (4.34)	194026 (6.34)	230956 (4.37)
2nd Decile	330961 (5.45)	224670 (7.34)	314474 (5.96)
3rd Decile	413922 (6.81)	253612 (8.29)	354286 (6.71)
4th Decile	475689 (7.83)	268197 (8.76)	414521 (7.86)
5th Decile	544180 (8.96)	288672 (9.43)	449456 (8.52)
6th Decile	588735 (9.69)	312223 (10.20)	507585 (9.62)
7th Decile	624079 (10.27)	332081 (10.85)	571981 (10.84)
8th Decile	695886 (11.45)	347234 (11.34)	649503 (12.31)
9th Decile	877523 (14.44)	391119 (12.78)	785011 (14.88)
10th Decile	1261493 (20.76)	449132 (14.67)	998672 (18.93)
Total	6076089 (100)	3060966 (100)	5276445 (100)

Note : Figures in brackets indicate the percentage share of income in each decile.

Appendix 2
Distribution of Cultivator Households by Size of Family (Income Decile)

(Amount in Rs.)

Income Decile	Upto 5 Members	6–7 Members	8–9 Members	9 & Above
Ist Decile	144154 (3.88)	186714 (5.45)	70611 (3.43)	213757 (4.10)
2nd Decile	210163 (5.66)	232265 (6.78)	96613 (4.69)	308135 (5.91)
3rd Decile	239460 (6.44)	251397 (7.33)	119970 (5.82)	361851 (6.95)
4th Decile	324473 (8.73)	269323 (7.86)	129044 (6.26)	428096 (8.22)
5th Decile	263533 (7.09)	305364 (8.91)	144337 (7.00)	473362 (9.09)
6th Decile	356244 (9.59)	339278 (9.90)	177983 (8.64)	523936 (10.06)
7th Decile	398838 (10.73)	357885 (10.44)	200626 (9.74)	605347 (11.62)
8th Decile	474412 (12.77)	407480 (11.89)	223226 (10.83)	658864 (12.65)
9th Decile	558552 (15.03)	463521 (13.52)	338480 (16.43)	711863 (17.74)
10th Decile	746264 (20.08)	614311 (17.92)	559778 (27.16)	923990 (17.74)
Total	3716093 (100)	3427538 (100)	2060668 (100)	5209201 (100)

Note : Figures in brackets indicate the percentage share of income in each decile.

Appendix 3
Distribution of Cultivator Households by Number of Earner (Decile)

(Amount in Rs.)

Income Decile	1 Earner	2 Earners	3 Earners	4 Earners	5 & Above
Ist Decile	64566 (5.45)	214846 (4.83)	112182 (3.66)	123366 (4.49)	180383 (6.08)
2nd Decile	88451 (7.47)	262844 (5.91)	157588 (5.14)	151071 (5.50)	202481 (6.82)
3rd Decile	95454 (8.06)	299843 (6.75)	184872 (6.03)	179029 (6.52)	218371 (7.36)
4th Decile	103692 (8.76)	334542 (7.53)	227094 (7.40)	198581 (7.23)	230755 (7.77)
5th Decile	116587 (9.84)	376987 (8.48)	275223 (8.97)	225785 (8.22)	251637 (8.48)
6th Decile	120627 (10.18)	435220 (9.79)	310866 (10.13)	236554 (8.61)	296150 (9.97)
7th Decile	126200 (10.65)	479217 (10.78)	332426 (10.84)	279836 (10.19)	342286 (11.53)
8th Decile	138294 (11.68)	533220 (11.99)	380851 (12.41)	354385 (12.90)	378575 (12.75)
9th Decile	159116 (13.43)	649519 (14.61)	470256 (15.33)	404400 (14.73)	421428 (14.19)
10th Decile	171502 (14.48)	859548 (19.33)	616193 (20.09)	593594 (21.61)	447007 (15.05)
Total	1184489 (100)	4445786 (100)	3067551 (100)	2746601 (100)	2969073 (100)

Note : Figures in brackets indicate the percentage share of income in each decile.

Appendix 4
Distribution of Cultivator Households by Educationwise and Income Level (Decile)

(Amount in Rs.)

Income Decile	No Formal Education	Primary	Middle	Matric	Graduate and Above
Ist Decile	278823 (3.31)	86920 (5.49)	76282 (4.91)	116436 (5.73)	13565 (1.64)
2nd Decile	388775 (4.62)	102265 (6.46)	98716 (6.35)	134696 (6.63)	20250 (2.45)
3rd Decile	477551 (5.67)	110703 (6.99)	107430 (6.91)	149378 (7.36)	30330 (3.67)
4th Decile	560608 (6.66)	131603 (8.31)	118215 (7.61)	160513 (7.90)	30427 (3.68)
5th Decile	645925 (7.67)	144484 (9.12)	138579 (8.92)	171230 (8.43)	48044 (5.81)
6th Decile	742093 (8.82)	153216 (9.67)	148325 (9.55)	200964 (9.90)	59804 (7.23)
7th Decile	894868 (10.63)	179866 (11.35)	161617 (10.40)	211906 (10.44)	117886 (14.26)
8th Decile	1076085 (12.78)	188360 (11.89)	186195 (11.98)	234218 (11.53)	136415 (16.50)
9th Decile	1537446 (18.27)	204432 (12.90)	234366 (15.08)	284214 (14.00)	171925 (20.80)
10th Decile	1815795 (21.57)	282287 (17.82)	284187 (18.29)	367187 (18.08)	198095 (23.96)
Total	8417969 (100)	1584136 (100)	1553912 (100)	2030742 (100)	826741 (100)

Note : Figures in brackets indicate the percentage share of income in each decile.

Appendix 5
Distribution of Cultivator Households by Age of Cheif Earner (Income Decile)

(Amount in Rs.)

Income Class	Upto 25 Years	23-30 Years	31-35 Years	36-40 Years	41-45 Years	46-50 Years	51-50 Years	56 & Above
Ist Decile	46558 (6.50)	116751 (4.99)	167382 (5.59)	94750 (4.55)	65155 (4.06)	100197 (6.06)	48130 (4.12)	107919 (5.82)
2nd Decile	49881 (6.96)	150610 (6.44)	197519 (6.60)	106340 (5.10)	94540 (5.88)	113929 (6.89)	58021 (4.97)	127140 (6.86)
3rd Decile	57026 (7.96)	171170 (7.32)	221952 (7.42)	121874 (5.85)	110001 (6.85)	131293 (7.94)	68643 (5.88)	137188 (7.40)
4th Decile	6372[illegible] (8.89)	186187 (7.96)	239507 (8.00)	135086 (6.48)	132396 (8.24)	146229 (8.84)	86816 (7.44)	144714 (7.81)
5th Decile	72026 (10.05)	207761 (8.89)	269683 (9.01)	155975 (7.49)	149176 (9.29)	151699 (9.17)	101817 (8.73)	156791 (8.46)
6th Decile	76172 (10.63)	226185 (9.67)	300571 (10.04)	180505 (8.66)	161585 (10.06)	159871 (9.66)	111805 (9.58)	176006 (9.49)
7th Decile	81876 (11.42)	251324 (10.74)	326180 (10.90)	205804 (9.88)	178065 (11.08)	176543 (10.67)	132315 (11.34)	218131 (11.77)
8th Decile	83394 (11.63)	292434 (12.50)	359611 (12.02)	239027 (11.47)	205304 (12.78)	199203 (12.04)	165280 (14.16)	230395 (12.43)
9th Decile	88472 (12.34)	318512 (13.62)	404348 (13.51)	313617 (15.05)	231254 (14.39)	218788 (13.22)	187044 (16.03)	259156 (13.98)
10th Decile	97646 (13.62)	417909 (17.87)	505874 (16.91)	530688 (25.47)	279084 (17.37)	256507 (15.51)	207178 (17.75)	296285 (15.98)
Total	716771 (100)	2338843 (100)	2992627 (100)	2083666 (100)	1606560 (100)	1654259 (100)	1167049 (100)	1853725 (100)

Note : Figures in brackets indicate the percentage share of income in each decile.

Appendix 6
Distribution of Cultivator Households by Income Level

(Amount in Rs.)

Income Level	Small Farmers			Medium Farmers		
	Average Income	Percentage Share in Household Population	Percentage Share in Income	Average Income	Percentage Share in Household Population	Percentage Share in Income
1	2	3	4	5	6	7
0-10000	7368.20	2.73	0.70	—	—	—
10001-20000	16204.84	26.78	15.05	—	—	—
20001-30000	24726.57	33.33	28.59	24599.80	15.15	8.04
30001-40000	34274.03	18.58	22.08	34860.10	28.79	21.64
40001-50000	44807.03	9.29	14.44	45212.13	27.27	26.59
50001-60000	54138.50	6.56	12.31	55101.57	10.60	12.60
60001-70000	65953.33	1.64	3.75	63646.20	7.58	10.40
70001-80000	78368.00	0.55	1.48	74903.00	1.52	2.44
80001-90000	84306.00	0.54	1.60	86015.00	3.03	5.62
90001-Above	—	—	—	96983.00	6.06	12.67
Total	28833.03	100.00	100.00	46378.27	100.00	100.00

Appendix 6
Distribution of Cultivator Households by Income Level

(Amount in Rs.)

Income Level	Large Farmers			Total Farmers		
	Average Income	Percentage Share in Household Population	Percentage Share in Income	Average Income	Percentage Share in Household Population	Percentage Share in Income
	8	9	10	11	12	13
0-10000	—	—	—	7368.20	1.56	0.25
10001-20000	—	—	—	16204.84	15.31	5.51
20001-30000	28160.00	1.41	0.46	24756.65	22.50	12.37
30001-40000	34372.25	11.27	4.53	34469.46	19.06	14.59
40001-50000	43229.75	5.63	2.85	44832.59	12.19	12.13
50001-60000	54432.33	12.68	8.06	54473.71	8.75	10.58
60001-70000	64185.71	9.86	7.39	64359.40	4.69	6.70
70001-80000	75308.20	14.08	12.39	75529.42	3.75	6.29
80001-90000	84441.00	16.90	16.68	84641.87	4.69	8.81
90001-Above	144723.35	28.17	47.64	136766.63	7.50	22.77
Total	85578.72	100.00	100.00	45042.18	100.00	100.00

Appendix 7
Distribution of Cultivator Households by Income Level and Size of Family

(Amount in Rs.)

Income Level	Upto 5 Members			with 6-7 Members		
	Average Income	Percentage Share in Household Population	Percentage Share in Income	Average Income	Percentage Share in Household Population	Percentage Share in Income
1	2	3	4	5	6	7
0-10000	6734.75	3.28	0.72	9902.00	1.19	0.29
10001-20000	16168.97	27.05	14.36	16359.67	10.72	4.30
20001-30000	24904.83	28.69	23.46	24232.23	30.95	18.38
30001-40000	34409.23	18.03	20.37	24696.00	25.00	21.26
40001-50000	44422.50	11.48	16.74	45313.00	14.29	15.86
50001-60000	55575.25	6.56	11.96	53477.50	4.76	6.24
60001-70000	66667.50	1.64	3.59	64544.00	4.76	7.53
70001-80000	75349.50	1.63	4.05	74492.00	2.38	4.35
80001-90000	82910.00	0.82	2.23	82325.00	1.19	2.40
90001-Above	93445.00	0.82	2.51	166148.50	4.76	19.39
Total	30459.78	100.00	100.00	40804.02	100.00	100.00

(Continued...)

Appendix 7
Distribution of Cultivator Households by Income Level and Size of Family

(Amount in Rs.)

Income Level	with 8-9 Members			9 and above		
	Average Income	Percentage Share in Household Population	Percentage Share in Income	Average Income	Percentage Share in Household Population	Percentage Share in Income
	8	9	10	11	12	13
0-10000	—	—	—	—	—	—
10001-20000	16232.00	7.50	2.36	16132.00	5.41	1.24
20001-30000	24350.00	15.00	7.09	26934.00	6.76	2.58
30001-40000	33252.64	27.50	17.75	35891.29	9.46	4.83
40001-50000	45100.20	12.50	10.94	44662.37	10.81	6.86
50001-60000	52318.50	15.00	15.23	55284.10	13.51	10.61
60001-70000	62423.00	2.50	3.03	63932.12	10.81	9.82
70001-80000	77175.00	5.00	7.49	75386.67	8.11	8.68
80001-90000	83120.00	2.50	4.04	85106.08	16.21	19.61
90001-Above	132157.60	12.50	32.07	133112.39	18.92	35.77
Total	51516.70	100.00	100.00	70394.61	100.00	100.00

Appendix 8
Distribution of Cultivator Households by Income Level and No. of Earners

(Amount in Rs.)

Income Level	With 1 Earner			With 2 Earners			With 3 Earners		
	Average Income	Percentage Share in Household Population	Percentage Share in Income	Average Income	Percentage Share in Household Population	Percentage Share in Income	Average Income	Percentage Share in Household Population	Percentage Share in Income
1	2	3	4	5	6	7	8	9	10
0-10000	6143.33	8.11	1.56	9205.50	1.49	0.42	—	—	—
10001-20000	15874.50	21.62	10.72	16408.19	23.13	11.44	1537.17	9.84	3.01
20001-30000	25134.36	29.73	2.33	24186.59	27.61	20.13	25237.33	19.67	9.87
30001-40000	35170.20	13.51	14.85	34383.36	24.63	25.52	34548.00	9.84	6.76
40001-50000	41788.33	8.11	10.58	45605.08	8.96	12.31	4565.00	18.03	16.16
50001-60000	54503.50	10.81	18.41	55981.10	7.46	12.59	52563.44	14.75	15.42
60001-70000	67000.00	2.70	5.66	64640.33	2.24	4.36	62839.00	6.56	8.20
70001-80000	—	—	—	—	—	—	75690.86	11.48	17.27
80001-90000	82190.00	2.71	7.00	82062.50	1.49	3.69	86659.50	3.28	5.65
90001-Above	93445.00	2.70	7.89	106012.00	2.99	9.54	135444.25	6.55	17.66
Total	32013.22	100.00	100.00	33177.51	100.00	100.00	50287.72	100.00	100.00

(Continued...)

Appendix 8
Distribution of Cultivator Households by Income Level and No. of Earners

(Amount in Rs.)

Income Level	With 4 Earners			With 5 and above		
	Average Income	Percentage Share in Household Population	Percentage Share in Income	Average Income	Percentage Share in Household Population	Percentage Share in Income
	11	12	13	14	15	16
0-10000	—	—	—	—	—	—
10001-20000	16280.67	7.41	1.78	17204.00	2.17	0.58
20001-30000	24957.00	14.29	5.45	26417.83	13.04	5.34
30001-40000	34720.29	16.67	8.85	34180.50	21.74	11.51
40001-50000	45102.33	21.43	14.78	43552.25	8.70	5.87
50001-60000	56810.00	4.76	4.14	53582.67	6.52	5.41
60001-70000	65686.00	4.76	4.78	64388.40	10.87	10.84
70001-80000	76683.00	4.76	5.58	74383.67	6.52	7.52
80001-90000	82806.33	7.14	9.04	85836.43	15.22	20.24
90001-Above	156559.63	19.05	45.60	138664.57	15.22	32.69
Total	65395.26	100.00	100.00	64545.06	100.00	100.00

Table 9

Distribution of Cultivator Households by Income Level and Education of Chief Sarnet

(Amount in Rs.)

Income Level	Not formal education			Primary			Middle		
	Average Income	Percentage Share in Household Population	Percentage Share in Income	Average Income	Percentage Share in Household Population	Percentage Share in Income	Average Income	Percentage Share in Household Population	Percentage Share in Income
1	2	3	4	5	6	7	8	9	10
0-100000	7083.00	1.90	0.34	-	-	-	-	-	-
10001-20000	16232.50	15.92	6.17	16048.00	9.09	3.04	15978.32	9.37	3.09
20001-30000	25045.42	23.88	14.28	23395.00	21.21	10.34	25421.71	21.88	11.45
30001-40000	14402.73	18.41	15.12	34800.29	21.22	15.38	34840.17	18.75	13.45
40001-50000	44757.96	11.44	12.23	46798.16	18.18	17.72	43952.83	18.75	16.97
50001-60000	54616.83	8.96	11.68	54149.25	12.12	13.67	55011.00	6.25	7.08
60001-70200	64401.50	4.96	7.65	-	-	-	65810.50	6.25	8.47
70001-80000	74937.78	4.47	8.01	79135.00	3.03	4.39	76389,00	6.25	9.83
80001-90000	84227.78	4.48	9.00	82190.00	6.06	10.38	88742.00	6.25	11.42
90001-Above	118736.45	5.47	15.52	129241.33	9.09	24.48	141681.00	6.25	18.24
Total	41880.44	100.00	100.00	48004.12	100.00	100.00	48559.75	100.00	100.00

Table 9

Distribution of Cultivator Households by Income Level and Education of Chief Sarnet

(Amount in Rs.)

Income Level	Matric			Graduate and Above		
	Average Income	Percentage Share in Household Population	Percentage Share in Income	Average Income	Percentage Share in Household Population	Percentage Share in Income
	11	12	13	14	15	16
0 - 10000	8509.00	2.27	0.42	-	-	-
10001 - 20000	16496.10	22.73	8.12	13565.00	10.00	1.64
20001 - 30000	24259.11	20.45	10.75	20250.00	10.00	2.45
30001 - 40000	35148.44	20.45	15.58	30378.50	20.00	7.35
40001 - 50000	42162.67	6.82	6.23	48044.00	10.00	5.81
50001 - 60000	51918.67	6.82	7.67	59804.00	10.00	7.23
60001 - 70000	63251.67	6.82	9.34	-	-	-
70001 - 80000	-	-	-	-	-	-
80001 - 90000	84857.00	4.55	8.36	-	-	-
90001 - Above	170222.75	9.09	33.53	156080.25	40.00	75.52
Total	46153.23	100.00	100.00	82674.10	100.00	100.00

Table 10

Distribution of Cultivator Households by Income Level and Age of Chief Earner

(Amount in Rs.)

Income Level	Average Income	Upto 25 Years Percentage Share in Household Population	Percentage Share in Income	Average Income	26-30 Years Percentage Share in Household Population	Percentage Share in Income	Average Income	31-35 Years Percentage Share in Household Population	Percentage Share in Income
1	2	3	4	5	6	7	8	9	10
0 - 10000	-	-	-	7926.50	3.64	0.68	9205.50	3.03	9.6
10001 - 20000	15157.71	29.17	14.80	16432.67	10.91	4.22	16425.91	16.67	6.00
20001 - 30000	25851.67	25.00	21.64	25068.87	27.27	16.08	24722.20	22.73	12.30
30001 - 40000	34132.00	33.33	38.10	34691.60	18.18	14.83	34616.91	16.67	12.70
40001 - 50000	44745.00	4.17	6.24	45234.50	10.91	11.60	44597.42	18.18	17.80
50001 - 60000	58370.00	4.16	8.14	53272.00	12.73	15.94	56596.00	6.06	7.50
60001 - 70000	-	-	-	66350.00	1.82	2.84	65258.00	4.54	6.50
70001 - 80000	79386.00	4.17	11.08	77049.50	3.63	6.59	75796.00	1.51	2.50
80001 - 90000	-	-	-	85356.33	5.45	10.95	82190.00	3.03	5.40
90001 - Above	-	-	-	126872.00	5.46	16.27	168881.80	7.58	28.20
Total	29865.46	100.00	100.00	42524.42	100.00	100.00	45342.83	100.00	100.00

(Continued...)

Table 10
Distribution of Cultivator Households by Income Level and Age of Chief Earner

(Amount in Rs.)

Income Level	Upto 25 Years			26-30 Years			31-35 Years		
	Average Income	Percentage Share in Household Population	Percentage Share in Income	Average Income	Percentage Share in Household Population	Percentage Share in Income	Average Income	Percentage Share in Household Population	Percentage Share in Income
	11	12	13	14	15	16	17	18	19
0-10000	-	-	-	2577.00	3.03	0.16	-	-	-
10001 - 20000	16994.08	23.53	9.79	15881.33	9.09	2.97	15786.40	14.29	4.77
20001 - 30000	24551.08	25.49	15.32	23825.60	15.15	7.41	25520.40	14.29	7.71
30001 - 40000	34992.90	19.61	16.79	35780.67	18.18	13.36	33240.78	25.71	18.08
40001 - 50000	45090.50	11.76	12.98	44199.40	15.16	13.76	45398.40	14.29	13.72
50001 - 60000	56725.00	3.92	5.44	54418.33	9.09	10.16	54335.33	8.57	9.85
60001 - 70000	66135.50	3.92	6.35	61986.67	9.09	11.58	64394.00	5.71	7.89
70001 - 80000	-	-	-	74235.00	6.06	9.24	73173.50	5.71	8.85
80001 - 90000	83973.50	3.92	8.06	84695.00	6.06	10.54	86161.00	5.71	10.42
90001 - Above	131608.25	7.85	25.27	111485.00	9.09	20.82	155551.50	5.72	18.81
Total	40856.10	100.00	100.00	48683.63	100.00	100.00	47264.54	100.00	100.00

(Continued...)

Table 10
Distribution of Cultivator Households by Income Level and Age of Chief Earner

(Amount in Rs.)

Income Level	Average Income	51-55 Years Percentage Share in Household Population	Percentage Share in Income	Average Income	56 & above Percentage Share in Household Population	Percentage Share in Income
	20	2	22	23	24	25
0 - 10000	-	-	-	-	-	-
10001 - 20000	15856.00	1.36	4.76	15572.75	11.43	3.36
20001 - 30000	23214.25	7.96	19.05	24639.11	25.71	11.96
30001 - 40000	32182.00	5.51	9.52	34747.00	14.29	9.37
40001 - 50000	44654.50	15.31	19.05	-	-	-
50001 - 60000	55015.50	9.43	9.53	52977.33	17.14	17.15
60001 - 70000	62423.00	5.35	4.76	64608.33	8.57	10.46
70001 - 80000	76683.00	13.14	9.52	74444.50	5.71	8.03
80001 - 90000	87565.00	15.00	9.52	82195.00	5.72	8.87
90001 - Above	104801.33	26.94	14.29	142744.75	11.43	30.80
Total	55573.76	100.00	100.00	52963.57	100.00	100.00

Table 11
Distribution of Cultivators Households by Assets
(Assets Decile)

(Amount in Rs.)

Asset Decile	Large Farmers	Medium Farmers	Small Farmers
Ist Decile	4541498 (4.56)	3006914 (6.97)	2059706 (4.23)
2nd Decile	5667268 (5.69)	3376809 (7.83)	3020716 (6.20)
3rd Decile	6086188 (6.11)	3551874 (8.24)	3516706 (7.22)
4th Decile	6620133 (6.65)	3849024 (8.92)	3980546 (8.17)
5th Decile	7223668 (7.26)	4061214 (9.42)	4370546 (8.97)
6th Decile	7922743 (7.96)	4228294 (9.80)	4650747 (9.54)
7th Decile	9333138 (9.37)	4352754 (10.09)	5062490 (10.39)
8th Decile	11408593 (11.46)	4635594 (10.75)	5630016 (11.55)
9th Decile	14642873 (14.71)	5069706 (11.76)	6389991 (13.11)
10th Decile	26119838 (26.23)	6995304 (16.22)	10046406 (20.62)
Total	99566940 (100)	43127487 (100)	48727869 (100)

Note: Figures in parentheses indicate the percentage share of income in each decile.

Table 12

Distribution of Cultivator Households by Asset Level and Size of Family (Asset - Decile)

(Amont in Rs.)

Asset Decile	Upto 5 members	6-7 Members	8-9 Members	9 & Above
Ist Decile	1837700 (3.81)	1978482 (4.64)	475180 (1.63)	2648661 (3.72)
2nd Decile	2457300 (5.09)	2481922 (5.81)	825880 (2.82)	3242395 (4.55)
3rd Decile	2848980 (5.90)	2749066 (6.44)	977030 (3.34)	3921116 (5.51)
4th Decile	3217530 (6.66)	2964458 (6.95)	1172600 (4.07)	5235966 (7.35)
5th Decile	3498350 (7.25)	3326294 (7.79)	1410900 (4.83)	6159143 (8.65)
6th Decile	3944004 (8.17)	4042904 (9.47)	1895205 (6.48)	6873631 (9.65)
7th Decile	4426835 (9.17)	4555984 (10.67)	2794450 (9.56)	7914666 (11.11)
8th Decile	6002475 (12.43)	5177074 (12.13)	3838985 (13.13)	9377566 (13.17)
9th Decile	7940280 (16.45)	6303929 (14.77)	4567150 (15.62)	11285541 (15.84)
10th Decile	12100085 (25.07)	9105924 (21.33)	11278250 (38.58)	14568376 (20.45)
Total	48273539 (100)	42686065(100)	29235630 (100)	71227062 (100)

Note: Figúres in parentheses indicate the percentage share of income in each decile.

Table 13

Distribution of Cultivator Households by Assets Level and Number of Earners (Asset Decile)

(Amount in Rs.)

Asset Decile	1 Earner	2 Earner	3 Earner	4 Earner	5 & Above
Ist Decile	1268125 (7.09)	1968010 (3.87)	1397398 (2.83)	1401735 (4.17)	2461062 (6.20)
2nd Decile	1401975 (7.83)	2622180 (5.16)	1737558 (3.52)	175990 (5.24)	2689962 (6.78)
3rd Decile	1507325 (8.43)	3051840 (6.00)	1975608 (4.00)	1924590 (5.70)	2773162 (6.99)
4th Decile	1656975 (9.26)	3412170 (6.71)	2236598 (4.53)	2225940 (6.62)	3093552 (7.80)
5th Decile	1709925 (9.56)	3775264 (7.42)	1747028 (5.56)	2825370 (8.40)	3732052 (9.4)
6th Decile	1753025 (9.80)	4460010 (8.77)	3878598 (7.86)	3163340 (9.41)	4198412 (10.5)
7th Decile	1826645 (10.21)	5262595 (10.35)	5329598 (10.80)	3580370 (10.65)	4606227 (11.6)
8th Decile	1976275 (11.04)	6493420 (12.77)	7.067788 (14.31)	4317545 (12.84)	4797472 (12.0)
9th Decile	2211175 (12.35)	8180927 (16.09)	9186738 (18.61)	5396115 (16.05)	5358372 (13.5)
10th Decile	2585105 (14.44)	11627550 (22.86)	13816448 (27.98)	7025820 (20.90)	5967322 (15.0)
Total	17896580 (100)	50853946 (100)	49373360 (100)	33620815 (100)	39677596 (100)

Note: Figures in parentheses indicate the percentage share asset.

Table 14

Distribution of Cultivator Households by Assets and Education wise (Asset Decile)
(Amount in Rs.)

Asset Decile	No Formal Education	Primary	Middle	Matric	Graduate and above
Ist Decile	2720510 (2.55)	1220668 (5.30)	1006895 (4.56)	1432354 (5.92)	189600 (1.23)
2nd Decile	4025310 (3.77)	1398178 (6.07)	1170400 (5.30)	1717374 (7.09)	216900 (1.40)
3rd Decile	4969280 (4.66)	1484078 (6.44)	1290800 (5.84)	1811664 (7.48)	273950 (1.77)
4th Decile	5554870 (5.21)	1631612 (7.08)	1509850 (6.83)	1897814 (7.84)	354650 (2.30)
5th Decile	6512855 (6.11)	1762998 (7.65)	1802460 (8.15)	1954724 (8.07)	629300 (4.08)
6th Decile	8027690 (7.53)	2302683 (10.00)	2070640 (9.37)	2026644 (8.37)	944100 (6.11)
7th Decile	11018560 (10.33)	2500428 (10.86)	2389530 (10.81)	2323674 (9.60)	1430850 (9.27)
8th Decile	14274755 (13.39)	2885143 (12.53)	2735757 (12.38)	2729699 (11.28)	2326400 (15.07)
9th Decile	18906280 (17.73)	3533528 (15.34)	2923210 (13.23)	3334794 (13.78)	4088500 (26.48)
10th Decile	30628095 (28.72)	4314428 (18.73)	5201135 (23.53)	1980479 (20.57)	4986500 (32.29)
Total	106617905 (100)	23033744 (100)	22400677 (100)	24209220 (100)	15440750 (100)

Note: Figures in parentheses indicate the percentage share of asset.

Table 15
Distribution of Cultivator Households by Assets and Education wise (Asset Decile)

(Amount in Rs.)

Asset Decile	Upto 25 yrs	26-30 yrs	31-35 yrs	36-40 yrs	41-45 yrs	46-50 yrs	51-55 yrs	56 & above
Ist Decile	665702 (6.02)	1254775 (4.72)	2270178 (5.80)	1000090 (3.76)	989549 (4.43)	1325205 (6.15)	460220 (3.61)	1894822
2nd Decile	782962 (7.08)	1746425 (6.57)	2475638 (6.33)	1263450 (4.75)	1120129 (5.02)	1495875 (6.94)	599430 (4.70)	2060812
3rd Decile	809882 (7.32)	1867265 (7.02)	27.2968 (6.91)	1430230 (5.38)	1183979 (5.30)	1551565 (7.19)	681080 (5.34)	2231262
4th Decile	876652 (7.93)	1950805 (7.34)	2854008 (7.30)	1583430 (5.96)	1470239 (6.59)	1647135 (7.64)	785580 (6.16)	2488262
5th Decile	949392 (8.59)	2087405 (7.85)	3075348 (7.86)	1674990 (6.30)	1726709 (7.73)	1737035 (8.05)	1042280 (8.17)	2678812
6th Decile	1072802 (9.70)	2343180 (8.82)	3662393 (9.36)	1792814 (6.75)	2265879 (10.05)	1792985 (8.31)	1157280 (9.08)	2922872
7th Decile	1182552 (10.70)	2565635 (9.65)	4291003 (10.97)	2254330 (8.48)	2623229 (11.75)	2040865 (9.46)	1257780 (9.86)	3338512
8th Decile	1364852 (12.34)	3387995 (12.75)	4856493 (12.41)	2786625 (10.49)	3004119 (13.46)	2732615 (12.67)	1386310 (10.87)	3611012
9th Decile	1560602 (14.11)	4446595 (16.73)	5760658 (14.73)	4449002 (16.74)	3308999 (14.82)	3150935 (14.61)	2324780 (18.23)	4755662
10th Decile	1792602 (16.21)	4932175 (18.55)	7177363 (18.33)	8343455 (31.39)	4632439 (20.75)	4092455 (18.98)	3057930 (23.98)	5456937
Total	11057970 (100)	26582255 (100)	39120050 (100)	26578416 (100)	22325300 (100)	21566670 (100)	12752670 (100)	31438965

Note: Figures in parentheses indicate the percentage share of asset.

Table 16
Distribution of Cultivator Households by Asset Level in Haryana

(Amount in Rs.)

Income Level	Small Farmers Average Income	Small Farmers Percentage Share in Household Population	Small Farmers Percentage Share in Income	Medium Farmers Average Income	Medium Farmers Percentage Share in Household Population	Medium Farmers Percentage Share in Income
1	2	3	4	5	6	7
0 - 100000	83673.64	6.01	1.89	-	-	-
100001-200000	163613.20	27.32	16.79	-	-	-
200001-300000	245605.65	40.99	37.80	-	-	-
300001-400000	337382.50	16.40	20.77	345478.33	9.09	4.81
400001-500000	436842.00	2.73	4.48	443087.50	27.27	18.49
500001-600000	551510.00	1.64	3.40	549009.47	28.79	24.19
600001-700000	648150.00	1.09	2.66	636023.38	12.12	11.80
700001-800000	730566.67	1.64	4.50	743737.00	7.58	8.62
800001-900000	863800.00	1.09	3.54	-	-	-
900001-1000000	-	-	-	-	-	-
1000001-1500000	1015280.00	1.09	4.17	1259561.30	12.12	23.36
1500001-2000000	-	-	-	1611600.00	1.51	3.74
2000001-Above	-	-	-	2152900.00	1.52	4.99
Total	266272.51	100.00	100.00	653446.77	100.00	100.00

(Continued...)

Table 16

Distribution of Cultivator Households by Asset Level in Haryana

(Amount in Rs.)

Income Level	Small Farmers			Medium Farmers		
	Average Income	Percentage Share in Household Population	Percentage Share in Income	Average Income	Percentage Share in Household Population	Percentage Share in Income
	8	9	10	11	12	13
0-100000	-	-	-	83673.64	3.44	0.48
100001-200000	-	-	-	163613.20	15.62	4.27
200001-300000	207550.00	1.41	0.21	245104.92	23.75	9.73
300001-400000	-	-	-	338731.81	11.25	6.37
400001-500000	496155.00	1.41	0.50	443997.50	7.50	5.57
500001-600000	-	-	-	549350.45	6.87	6.31
600001-700000	644210.00	5.63	2.59	640094.79	4.38	4.68
700001-800000	747324.23	18.31	9.76	744076.19	6.56	8.16
800001-900000	858163.89	12.68	7.76	859188.64	3.44	4.94
900001-1000000	958875.63	11.27	7.70	958875.63	2.50	4.01
1000001-1500000	1201104.30	21.13	18.09	1204944.60	7.81	15.74
1500001-2000000	1744063.00	14.08	17.52	1732020.90	3.44	9.95
2000001-Above	3571950.50	14.08	35.87	3442945.90	3.44	19.79
Total	1402351.30	100.00	100.00	598194.67	100.00	100.00

Table 17
Distribution of Cultivator Households by Asset Level and Size of Family

(Amount in Rs.)

Income Level	Average Income	Upto 5 members Percentage Share in Household Population	Percentage Share in Income	Average Income	With 6-7 members Percentage Share in Household Population	Percentage Share in Income
1	2	3	4	5	6	7
0-100000	84500.00	4.92	1.05	79655.50	2.38	0.37
100001-200000	126166.43	22.95	9.41	163457.50	14.29	4.59
200001-300000	243807.33	29.50	18.18	246100.00	28.57	1.38
300001-400000	330473.24	13.93	11.64	358071.43	8.33	5.87
400001-500000	437306.00	4.10	4.53	449123.93	16.67	14.73
500001-600000	544206.50	8.20	11.27	556849.29	8.33	9.13
600001-700000	634243.33	2.46	3.94	639276.67	3.58	4.49
700001-800000	754933.75	6.56	12.51	747401.67	3.57	5.25
800001-900000	838287.50	1.64	3.47	864576.67	3.57	6.07
900001-1000000	970325.00	1.64	4.02	966185.00	2.38	4.52
1000001-1500000	1206375.00	1.64	5.00	1204360.00	3.57	8.46
1500001-2000000	1611600.00	0.82	3.34	1655256.70	3.57	11.63
2000001-Above	2809200.0	1.64	11.64	4701700.00	1.19	11.01
Total	395684.75	100.00	100.00	508167.44	100.00	100.00

(Contined...)

Table 17
Distribution of Cultivator Households by Asset Level and Size of Family

(Amount in Rs.)

Income Level	with 8-9 members			with 9 and above		
	Average Income	Percentage Share in Household Population	Percentage Share in Income	Average Income	Percentage Share in Household Population	Percentage Share in Income
	8	9	10	11	12	13
0-100000	81500.00	5.00	0.56	91100.00	1.35	0.13
100001-200000	174140.00	10.00	2.38	163658.33	8.11	1.38
200001-300000	248122.50	20.00	6.79	244941.25	10.81	2.75
300001-400000	336175.00	15.00	6.90	342125.00	8.11	2.88
400001-500000	422341.67	7.50	4.33	457325.00	2.70	1.28
500001-600000	-	-	-	549140.00	6.76	3.85
600001-700000	659860.00	7.50	6.77	632237.40	6.76	4.44
700001-800000	721525.00	5.00	4.94	737609.38	10.81	8.28
800001-900000	890850.00	0.25	3.05	857984.00	6.76	6.02
900001-1000000	970467.50	5.00	6.64	928525.00	2.70	2.61
1000001-1500000	1114870.00	12.50	19.07	1234895.70	20.27	26.01
1500001-2000000	1635000.00	0.25	5.59	1806643.30	8.11	15.22
2000001-Above	3214416.70	7.50	32.98	3581811.00	6.75	25.15
Total	730890.75	100.00	100.00	962527.86	100.00	100.00

Appendix 18

Distribution of Cultivator Households by Asset Level and Number of Earner

(Amount in Rs.)

Asset Level	With 1 Earner			With 2 Earners			With 3 Earners		
	Average Asset	Percentage Share in Household Population	Percentage Share in Asset	Average Asset	Percentage Share in Household Population	Percentage Share in Asset	Average Asset	Percentage Share in Household Population	Percentage Share in Income
1	2	3	4	5	6	7	8	9	10
0-100000	80887.50	10.81	1.81	87718.33	4.48	1.03	70550.00	1.64	0.14
100001-200000	155300.00	16.22	5.21	162488.33	22.39	9.59	173564.29	11.47	2.46
200001-300000	238086.36	29.73	14.63	239123.65	25.37	15.99	250876.67	24.59	7.62
300001-400000	320125.00	10.81	7.15	341097.25	14.93	13.41	326062.50	6.56	2.64
400001-500000	442483.33	8.11	7.42	443146.67	8.95	10.46	436106.00	8.20	4.42
500001-600000	528790.00	5.41	5.91	553222.73	8.21	11.97	548025.00	3.28	2.22
600001-700000	-	-	-	646896.75	2.98	5.09	675700.00	3.28	2.74
700001-800000	740550.00	5.41	8.28	741897.00	3.73	7.29	731516.67	4.92	4.44
800001-900000	844500.00	2.70	4.72	859845.00	3.73	8.45	837515.00	3.28	3.39
900001-1000000	-	-	-	944100.00	0.75	1.86	978960.00	3.28	3.97
1000001-1500000	1206375.00	5.40	13.48	1184446.00	3.73	11.65	1219808.90	14.75	22.24
1500001-2000000	-	-	-	1635000.00	0.75	3.21	1769583.30	9.83	21.50
2000001-Above	2809200.00	5.40	31.39	-	-	-	3656400.00	4.92	22.25
Total	483691.35	100.00	100.00	379504.06	100.00	100.00	809399.34	100.00	100.00

(Continued...)

Table 18
Distribution of Cultivator Households by Asset Level and Number of Earner

(Amount in Rs.)

Asset Level	with 4 earners: Average Income	with 4 earners: Percentage Share in Household Population	with 4 earners: Percentage Share in Asset	with 5 & more earners: Average Income	with 5 & more earners: Percentage Share in Household Population	with 5 & more earners: Percentage Share in Asset
	11	12	13	14	15	16
0-100000	-	-	-	-	-	-
100001-200000	152690.00	7.14	1.36	175297.50	8.70	1.77
200001-300000	268964.29	16.67	5.60	248102.22	19.56	5.63
300001-400000	358741.67	14.29	6.40	317600.00	4.35	1.60
400001-500000	470500.00	2.38	14.00	453233.33	6.52	3.43
500001-600000	560295.00	9.52	6.67	535150.00	6.52	4.04
600001-700000	628070.00	9.52	7.47	627515.00	8.70	6.33
700001-800000	752980.00	9.53	8.96	746935.00	15.22	13.18
800001-900000	890850.00	2.38	2.65	870735.00	4.35	4.39
900001-1000000	970645.00	7.14	8.66	928525.00	4.35	4.68
1000001-1500000	1294518.80	9.52	15.40	1126456.00	10.87	14.19
1500001-2000000	1621126.70	7.15	14.47	1936350.00	2.17	4.88
2000001-Above	3523712.50	4.76	20.96	3559345.00	8.69	35.88
Total	800495.60	100.00	100.00	862556.41	100.00	100.00

Appendix 19
Distribution of Cultivator Households by, Asset Level and Education of Chief Earners

(Amount in Rs.)

Asset Level	Not formal Education Average Asset	Percentage Share in Household Population	Percentage Share in Asset	Primary Average Asset	Percentage Share in Household Population	Percentage Share in Asset	Middle Average Asset	Percentage Share in Household Population	Percentage Share in Income
1	2	3	4	5	6	7	8	9	10
0-100000	79225.00	2.99	0.45	93320.00	3.03	0.41	96490.00	3.12	0.44
100001-200000	159886.00	14.92	4.50	171506.67	18.18	4.47	169136.00	15.63	3.82
200001-300000	249993.40	24.87	11.72	251307.33	18.18	6.54	239362.50	12.50	4.33
300001-400000	342217.59	13.43	8.66	315460.00	6.06	2.74	326800.00	9.37	4.43
400001-500000	439842.50	5.97	4.95	485135.00	9.09	6.32	439030.00	12.50	7.95
500001-600000	552266.43	6.97	7.25	551050.00	9.09	7.18	545610.00	9.37	7.41
600001-700000	633084.44	4.48	5.34	612780.00	3.03	2.66	673829.00	9.38	9.15
700001-800000	745833.21	6.97	9.79	712542.50	6.06	6.19	761777.50	12.50	13.79
800001-900000	864038.57	3.48	5.47	857825.00	6.06	7.45	-	-	-
900001-1000000	957194.00	2.49	4.49	970600.00	3.03	4.21	970335.00	3.13	4.39
1000001-1500000	1190921.50	8.46	18.99	1231212.50	12.13	21.38	-	-	-
1500001-2000000	1739501.30	3.98	13.05	1522970.00	3.03	6.61	1806625.00	6.25	16.35
2000001-Above	2740625.00	1.49	5.14	5492130.00	3.03	23.84	3087762.50	6.25	27.94
Total	530536.54	100.00	100.00	697992.24	100.00	100.00	690646.16	100.00	100.00

(Continued...)

Table 19

Distribution of Cultivator Households by Asset Level and Education of Chief Earners

(Amount in Rs.)

Asset Level	with 4 earners			with 5 & more earners		
	Average Income	Percentage Share in Household Population	Percentage Share in Asset	Average Income	Percentage Share in Household Population	Percentage Share in Asset
	11	12	13	14	15	16
0-100000	85083.33	6.81	1.05	-	-	-
100001-200000	164970.00	18.18	5.45	189600.00	10	1.22
200001-300000	226582.86	31.82	13.10	245425.00	20	3.18
300001-400000	329500.00	6.82	4.08	354650.00	10	2.30
400001-500000	433261.00	11.36	8.95	-	-	-
500001-600000	532000.00	4.55	4.40	-	-	-
600001-700000	-	-	-	629300.00	10	4.08
700001-800000	711740.00	2.27	2.94	-	-	-
800001-900000	843577.50	4.55	6.97	-	-	-
900001-1000000	-	-	-	944100.00	10	6.11
1000001-1500000	11740.83	6.82	14.55	1430850.00	10	9.27
1500001-2000000	-	-	-	-	-	-
2000001-Above	3107366.70	6.82	38.51	3800466.70	30	73.84
Total	550209.55	100.00	100.00	1544075.00	100	100.00

Table 20
Distribution of Cultivator Households by Asset Level and Age of Chief Earner

(Amount in Rs.)

Asset Level	Upto 26 years Average Asset	Upto 26 years Percentage Share in Household Population	Upto 26 years Percentage Share in Asset	26-30 years Average Asset	26-30 years Percentage Share in Household Population	26-30 years Percentage Share in Asset	31-35 years Average Asset	31-35 years Percentage Share in Household Population	31-35 years Percentage Share in Asset
1	2	3	4	5	6	7	8	9	10
0-100000	81750.00	4.17	0.74	76733.33	5.45	0.87	-	-	-
100001-200000	178162.00	20.83	8.05	160447.50	7.27	2.41	156377.33	22.72	6.00
200001-300000	251648.00	20.83	11.38	239550.56	32.73	16.22	233247.86	21.21	8.35
300001-400000	374900.00	16.67	13.56	335363.89	16.36	11.35	345983.33	9.09	5.31
400001-500000	-	-	-	427346.67	5.45	4.82	457151.43	10.60	8.10
500001-600000	559033.33	12.50	15.17	531790.00	3.64	4.00	552525.00	7.58	7.06
600001-700000	643800.00	4.17	5.82	699250.00	1.82	2.63	607290.00	3.03	3.10
700001-800000	759633.33	12.50	20.61	746625.00	10.91	16.85	731162.00	7.58	9.34
800001-900000	-	-	-	852477.50	7.27	12.83	864122.50	3.03	4.42
900001-1000000	-	-	-	908300.00	1.82	3.42	970416.67	4.55	7.44
1000001-1500000	1204800.00	4.17	10.90	1135275.00	3.64	8.54	1175687.50	6.06	12.02
1500001-2000000	1522970.00	4.16	13.77	1936350.00	1.82	7.29	-	-	-
2000001-Above	-	-	-	2330350.00	1.82	8.77	3752566.70	4.55	28.78
Total	480748.75	100.00	100.00	483313.73	100.00	100.00	592728.03	100.00	100.00

(Continued...)

Table 20
Distribution of Cultivator Households by Asset Level and Age of Chief Earner

(Amount in Rs.)

Asset Level	Average Asset	36-40 years Percentage Share in Household Population	Percentage Share in Asset	Average Asset	41-45 years Percentage Share in Household Population	Percentage Share in Asset	Average Asset	46-50 years Percentage Share in Household Population	Percentage Share in Asset
	11	12	13	14	15	16	17	18	19
0-100000	87920.00	3.92	0.66	86130.00	6.06	0.77	93320.00	2.86	0.43
100001-200000	170759.00	19.61	6.42	148535.71	21.22	4.66	189795.00	5.72	1.76
200001-300000	253538.56	35.30	17.17	258786.67	9.09	3.48	247060.91	31.43	12.60
300001-400000	316985.00	3.92	2.39	304050.00	6.06	2.72	314870.00	14.29	7.30
400001-500000	433996.67	11.77	9.80	424730.00	3.03	1.90	429865.00	5.71	3.99
500001-600000	518522.50	3.92	2.90	536075.00	12.12	9.61	-	-	-
600001-700000	657068.50	3.92	4.95	655450.00	3.03	2.94	633120.00	11.43	11.74
700001-800000	-	-	-	752960.00	12.12	13.49	781500.00	2.86	3.62
800001-900000	832800.00	1.96	3.13	871706.67	9.09	11.71	865000.00	2.86	4.01
900001-1000000	959542.50	3.92	7.22	-	-	-	-	-	-
1000001-1500000	1096116.70	5.88	12.37	1219245.00	6.06	10.92	1132580.00	11.42	21.01
1500001-2000000	-	-	-	1567550.00	6.06	14.04	1808177.50	11.42	33.54
2000001-Above	2833975.00	5.88	31.99	2651900.00	6.06	23.76	-	-	-
Total	521145.41	100.00	100.00	676524.24	100.00	100.00	616190.57	100.00	100.00

(Continued...)

Table 20

Distribution of Cultivator Households by Asset Level and Age of Chief Earner

(Amount in Rs.)

Asset Level	51-55 years Average Asset	51-55 years Percentage Share in Household Population	51-55 years Percentage Share in Asset	56 & above years Average Asset	56 & above years Percentage Share in Household Population	56 & above years Percentage Share in Asset
	20	21	22	23	24	25
0-100000	96490.00	4.76	0.76	70550.00	2.86	0.22
100001-200000	196650.00	4.76	1.54	163136.67	17.14	3.11
200001-300000	236587.50	19.05	7.42	262760.00	8.57	2.50
300001-400000	309250.00	9.52	4.85	360941.67	17.14	6.89
400001-500000	466350.00	19.05	14.63	420000.00	2.86	1.34
500001-600000	560583.33	14.29	13.19	573103.33	8.57	5.47
600001-700000	628180.00	4.76	4.93	636725.00	5.71	4.05
700001-800000	-	-	-	708900.00	5.71	4.51
800001-900000	-	-	-	-	-	-
900001-1000000	971000.00	4.76	7.61	961370.00	2.86	3.06
1000001-1500000	135918.33	14.29	31.97	1268467.50	17.14	24.21
1500001-2000000	1670800.00	4.76	13.10	1777150.00	5.72	11.31
2000001-Above	-	-	-	5239315.00	5.72	33.33
Total	607270.00	100.00	100.00	898256.14	100.00	100.00

Index